ORGANIC VEGETABLE GARDENING

Beginner's Guide to Quickly Learn and Master How to Grow Your Own Vegetables and How to Start a Healthy Garden at Home

By
Rachel Martin

© Copyright 2019 by Rachel Martin - All rights reserved.

This content is provided with the sole purpose of providing relevant information on a specific topic for which every reasonable effort has been made to ensure that it is both accurate and reasonable. Nevertheless, by purchasing this content you consent to the fact that the author, as well as the publisher, are in no way experts on the topics contained herein, regardless of any claims as such that may be made within. As such, any suggestions or recommendations that are made within are done so purely for entertainment value. It is recommended that you always consult a professional prior to undertaking any of the advice or techniques discussed within.

This is a legally binding declaration that is considered both valid and fair by both the Committee of Publishers Association and the American Bar Association and should be considered as legally binding within the United States.

The reproduction, transmission, and duplication of any of the content found herein, including any specific or extended information will be done as an illegal act regardless of the end form the information ultimately takes. This includes copied versions of the work both physical, digital and audio unless express consent of the Publisher is provided beforehand. Any additional rights reserved.

Furthermore, the information that can be found within the pages described forthwith shall be considered both accurate and truthful when it comes to the recounting of facts. As such, any use, correct or incorrect, of the provided information will render the Publisher free of responsibility as to the actions taken outside of their direct purview. Regardless, there are zero scenarios where the original author or the Publisher can be deemed liable in any fashion for any damages or hardships that may result from any of the information discussed herein.

Additionally, the information in the following pages is intended only for informational purposes and should thus be thought of as universal. As befitting its nature, it is presented without assurance regarding its prolonged validity or interim quality. Trademarks that are mentioned are done without written consent and can in no way be considered an endorsement from the trademark holder.

TABLE OF CONTENTS

Introduction 1

Chapter 1 *The Basics of Why & How: Organic 101* 2

Chapter 2 *Soil And Seeds: Getting Started* 11

Chapter 3 *Vegetable Victory: Choosing the Best Plants for Your Garden* 22

Chapter 4 *Preparing for Pests: Embrace the Inevitable* 35

Chapter 5 *Healthy Harvest: Weeding, Pruning, Using* 41

Chapter 6 *Preserving Your Produce: Strategies for Zero Waste Gardening* 61

Chapter 7 *Sustaining The Seasons: Making The Best Of Your Garden Year Round* 72

Chapter 8 *Imagining Your Impact: The Final Payoff* 77

Conclusion 82

Description 83

INTRODUCTION

Never has the time been riper to embark upon the joyful challenge of growing your own vegetables—organically, healthfully—at home. This book will guide you through the process, from the basics of why and how to the fruitful activities of harvesting and preserving.

First, we will begin with a quick overview of *what* it means to garden organically, *why* it is important, and *how* to do it simply and skillfully. From there, we will tackle some basics: preparing the soil and sourcing the seeds get the garden off the ground, literally. Next, determining what vegetables and herbs to grow is obviously fundamental and, certainly, a big part of the fun of gardening; customizing your garden is one of the pleasures of having one. Once the basics are in place, planning for the inevitable—if you build it, the pests will come—becomes a necessary task, albeit one more welcome than it might at first seem. As you start to garden, you will find that combating garden nuisances brings out the innovative best in many of us.

Next, we will examine the best ways to keep the garden healthy throughout the growing season and, more importantly, how to harvest and utilize your bounty. This includes some ideas for simple recipes and longer term preservation: unearthing a bag of vine-ripened roasted tomatoes from your freezer in the middle of February is akin to harnessing the summer sunshine. And, of course, sustaining a garden throughout all four seasons is the ideal.

Last, a look back on what has been accomplished and the impact it creates in our lives and for our world: From the back yard to the table, growing your own vegetable garden is a wonderful way to sustain yourself and all those you love.

CHAPTER 1
The Basics of Why & How: Organic 101

What Is Organic Gardening?

The U.S. Department of Agriculture, under the auspices of the National Organic Program (NOP), determines the definition and regulation of how the term organic is used and labeled in our food supply. To put it simply, the term organic indicates foods that have been grown or raised without the use of genetically modified organisms (GMOs), sewer sludge—many industrial farms water their crops with treated sewage runoff—and, in the case of meat products, irradiation.

The NOP also requires organic crops to be grown without the use of petroleum-based or otherwise synthesized fertilizers and pesticides, though these rules are subject to modification every five years, and the NOP has come under criticism for allowing small amounts of synthetic materials to be used even under the label "organic." The NOP also oversees the nationwide certification program by which a farm attains the "certified organic" label. Be aware, however, that the certification process is lengthy and costly, so many smaller farms—such as those who sell at local farmers' markets—may in practice follow the regulations for growing organic crops but do not actually hold a certification. If you buy at local farmers' markets, which I urge you to do as most home gardeners cannot grow everything they might want for their table, simply ask your farmer what kind of chemicals and methods he or she uses at their farm. If a local farmer sprays a typical pesticide once a year, it is still far healthier than buying an industrially farmed product that is constantly sprayed.

For the home gardener, this all becomes pretty simple: in order to garden organically, you simply need to avoid synthetic fertilizers in favor of natural ones, such as compost (which will be discussed in the next chapter), and synthetic pesticides. The home gardener need not worry about sewer sludge, one assumes, though locating your garden away from neighborhood ponds or parks is always a good idea, as areas that are kept up by communities or government-run entities often use synthetic materials; avoiding runoff ensures that your garden maximizes its healthy, organic potential.

Why Garden Organically?

As most of us are very much aware, the ills of industrial agriculture are well documented. The use of petroleum-based fertilizers and pesticides are destructive to the environment—the soil, the air, groundwater—as well as being a non-renewable resource fraught with the political implications of how and where oil is obtained. In addition, most of us are aware that the health costs of eating produce laden with chemicals are certainly significant, especially so for children. As a pediatrician, I once knew put it bluntly: "I would not feed my children a non-organic apple."

There are other factors involved in the industrial production of our food supply that are also worth mentioning and should give us reason to rethink our food choices. Some prime examples include the simple matter of taste, the imprint of our carbon footprint, the danger of monocultures, the unknown threats levied by GMOs, and the unseen costs of human rights abuses.

- **Taste**: While many might argue that taste is subjective, a matter of personal opinion, when it comes to a homegrown, vine-ripened tomato, I defy anyone to compare it to a supermarket tomato and give an unfavorable review to the backyard version. Supermarket tomatoes have been bred for hardiness, so they can be harvested easily and shipped for long distances, not taste. They are most often picked off the vine while green—this allows for the use of machine harvesters which essentially knock the unripe tomatoes to the ground; ripe tomatoes would splat—and ship them in trucks that spray them with manufactured ethylene gas to artificially make them appear "ripe." What you are buying at the grocery store is an unripe, sour, bland tomato that has been mechanically coaxed into blushing slightly. While here the tomato provides the example, it can easily be extrapolated to include any number of vegetables and fruits that are grown for convenient consumption rather than satisfying flavor.

- **Carbon Footprint**: As the above example acknowledges, with industrial agriculture, shipping becomes of primary concern. Most of our produce is grown elsewhere unless you happen to live in parts of California or Florida. Thus, our fruits and vegetables are grown for hardiness not only with regard to disease or pests but also for their ability to withstand the rigors of shipping. So, the carbon footprint left behind by the average American table is quite concerning: fertilizers and pesticides used notwithstanding, the oil used in transport is staggering. In fact, industrial agriculture is considered to be the second largest contributor to greenhouse gases, second only to the energy industry.

- **Monocultures**: Another danger involved in the intensive farming that is the hallmark of industrial agriculture is the creation of monocultures. This is when a particular crop, usually one particular strain, is grown extensively over a large area of land. The traditional American farm consisted of many different crops, as well as livestock, working together in harmony: the fertilizer created by the livestock nurtured the variety of produce grown which, in turn, fed both the animals and the family. On contemporary industrial farms, one product is grown exclusively—think of the wheat fields of Kansas (now mostly soybean fields, actually), stretching as far as the eye can see. This is true not only of grain crops but also of tomatoes, apples, citrus, and many other varieties of produce. The danger in monocultures is that, when one kind of crop is grown intensively in one area, it depletes the soil of nutrients and becomes increasingly vulnerable to disease. For example, in recent years, we have seen banana crops—grown intensively in tropical regions—virtually wiped out in places because of disease: when one strain of banana, the Cavendish, supplanted most other strains, the crops became vulnerable to a quick-spreading fungal invasion. Monocultures are always at risk, on the verge of extinction.

- **Genetically Modified Organisms**: While the effects of the widespread use of genetically modified organisms (GMOs) are still largely unknown, the dangers that are present in the practice of monoculture farming are similar to that created by GMO farming, the susceptibility to disease and the depletion of the soil. In addition, the use of GMOs also brings with it a host of other potential threats, not least of them the invasiveness of some of these crops. For one example, Monsanto created a genetically modified corn crop that was so successful, its seeds invaded other fields in many areas, choking out the more traditional breeds. It should be noted that this particular strain of corn was bred to resist the weed killer, Roundup (called "Roundup ready," there are several crops that were genetically modified in this manner); this allowed farmers to spray their fields with weed killer throughout the growing season without harming the corn (or canola, or soybean, etc.). As well, Monsanto patents these products which means that farmers cannot use their seeds without paying for them—and must buy new seeds every year, as the plant is also bred to be sterile—and at least one farmer has been sued by the corporation because Roundup ready plants were found in his field, his seeds being contaminated by the GMO version. Thus, the increasingly widespread use of GMOs represents the continuing intensification of corporate control over our farms and crops, as well as posing potential threats to our health. The FDA does not require testing on humans before GMO crops are approved, and furthermore, does not require products containing GMOs to be labeled.

- **Labor Issues**: The last problematic symptom of the ills of industrial agriculture is one of the least talked about and largely unseen concerns, that of human rights abuses. While many of us are aware that a great deal of agricultural labor which has not been mechanized is done by migrants, few of us know of the conditions under which many of these laborers must endure. Many of the migrant laborers who work in the field could actually be considered indentured servants. These vulnerable men and women are lured onto farms with promises of decent pay for hard work, yet they find themselves trapped into paying exorbitant rents for shacks without running water or electricity while making just a few dollars a day. Bosses often give them "advances" on their meager pay so the laborers can purchase food or liquor, which leaves them in debt. There are also reports of physical abuse if workers do not move fast enough or work hard enough. A full account of what goes on at some farms is exposed in detail in Barry Estabrook's thorough account of the tomato-farming industry, *Tomatoland*.

All of that said, the advantages of home gardening organically seem clear: you can avoid the potential health risks of exposure to petrochemicals and the ethical conundrums involved in the practices of industrial agriculture all the while growing much tastier, more beautiful, and most satisfying food. The benefit to yourself, your family, and your environment cannot be overstated, and even the smallest of gardens have an outsized impact. So, let us tackle the logistics and get started today!

How to Garden Organically?

Even if you have never gardened, doing so organically is not terribly complicated, though knowing a few ground rules certainly eases the process. And, if you have gardened in the past but wish to do so a little more healthfully now, then the transition will be particularly easy. In the next chapter, we will start to look more specifically into the basics of *organic* gardening, but to begin, let us take a look at what we might need to think about to get a garden of any kind growing.

First, any good gardener worth his or her salt should invest in **quality tools**. Visit your local gardening emporium or, if necessary, for convenience and cost-effectiveness, a big box mart for advice and products. A handy list of some basic tools you will want to acquire follows.

- **Small Shed:** This may not be a necessary item for the lucky gardener with plenty of convenient, non-used garage space, but for many of us it will become a crucial item. If you garden in your backyard, as quite a lot of us do, with a garage in the front of the house, then a storage shed on the back porch can be a huge timesaver. Not only will everything be readily at hand, but this setup also allows for ease of organization. Sturdy plastic sheds can be purchased relatively inexpensively at any number of garden centers. I went without for my first two seasons of gardening and was amazed at the increase in my efficiency (along with a decrease in my irritation) by getting one and keeping it well organized.

- **GLOVES!:** This comes in at the top of my list because their importance cannot be overstated. It is difficult to garden with a missing fingernail or cuts all over your hands (though getting some dirt under the nails can make one feel accomplished). I'd recommend more than one kind of glove: a thin pair of washable gloves that allow for dexterity when planting seeds and fine weeding; some latex gloves for wet jobs or weeding amongst thorny plants; and a pair of heavy leather gloves for tough jobs like digging large holes, moving soil, or raking. If you have sensitive skin—cucumber and tomato vines are quite prickly—you might also want to invest in some elasticized arm protectors (or an old long-sleeved shirt and some sturdy rubber bands).

- **Shovels:** Round-headed shovels are best for all-purpose work, like digging holes and moving soil or compost. Make sure to get a sturdy one and keep it clean after use, to prolong its life. Steelheads are typically sturdier than aluminum.

- **Rakes:** There are two types of long-handled rakes useful for gardening in general: a lightweight leaf rake for raking leaves and grass clippings and a bow rake for leveling soil and spreading compost and mulch. For the vegetable gardener, a hand rake also comes in handy for close work, such as removing debris from around the base of a plant without damaging stalks or roots.

- **Hand Trowel:** This is used for digging small, precise holes for planting and close weeding. A hori-hori knife of Japanese origin can be used in the same way as a hand trowel, with the added advantage of having a saw blade when needed to divide young plants.

- **Shears and Scissors:** a good pair of shears is especially useful at the end of the gardening season, to cut down any dead or dying vines; it is also great for pruning should you have larger items in your garden, such as hedges, to tackle.

Designating a sturdy pair of scissors for garden work is indispensable for clipping tender herbs and pruning back delicate plants.

- **Pruners:** while a solid set of shears and scissors works for most vegetable gardening, a sturdy pruner is sometimes necessary when growing larger plants and bushes. It can be used to cut thicker branches, and if you get a long-handled one, to prune trees.

- **Transplant Spade:** this tool is like a larger, longer handled trowel and saves the back when transplanting a lot of young plants at one time. Recommended if you intend your garden to be large.

- **Digging Fork:** this is used to move loose soil and turn it over. There are short handled forks and long-handled forks. I tend to use a short handled one for close work while a bow rake suits most other tasks.

- **Watering Solutions:** The most basic watering tool for the casual backyard gardener is the garden hose; and this, certainly, will work for any gardener with the time to spend watering thoroughly. It served me well, along with a handheld watering can and a water breaker attachment (which provides a gentle even flow of water to avoid damaging plants), for a few years. But, when I finally invested in a soaker system—or, drip irrigation—I was pleased and relieved: just turning on the hose for 30 minutes in the morning (and another 30 in the early evening during hot weather) did the trick while I could do other things. This is a more expensive option, but it is well worth it for the serious home gardener, especially if you live in drought-prone areas.

- **Composting Solutions:** If you truly want to garden organically, you absolutely must invest in some sort of composter. There are numerous models on the market with prices varying from the modest to the expensive, from the small indoor to the large outdoor. However, while most of these models are fuss-free and efficient, it is also possible to make your own composter with a few simple items. In the next chapter, the basics of composting are discussed in detail.

Second, it helps for the home gardener to have some reliable resources on hand—such as this book!—to consult for advice and troubleshooting. Besides this book, below is a list of some other resources available to most home gardeners.

- **Local Stores:** In the age of online shopping, which admittedly cannot be paralleled in terms of ease and convenience, it is still important to remember that your local store can give specific and useful advice. Typically, the proprietor knows the area and what works best in said area. As well, frequenting a particular business with regularity forms a lasting relationship, wherein a past purchase leads to a present conversation which prevents a future problem.

- **Farmers' Markets:** If you have the pleasure to enjoy a farmers' market in your area, it behooves you to frequent it and become friendly with your local farmers. Most farmers at the market are huge proponents of backyard gardens, seeing them not as competition but as bedfellows in a project to create a healthier and more environmentally friendly world. As well, they are purveyors of much wisdom and will often happily pass said advice along. In addition, many farmers welcome visitors to the farm and, if your market boasts any organic farm stands, I urge you to visit and to ask many questions. They can assist you in almost every aspect of farming, from what and when to plant, to how much and when to water, to combating disease and pests, to harvesting and preparing what you grow. And, you can procure many lovely vegetables and fruits (or humanely produced meat, eggs, milk, cheese, honey) that you don't happen to have in your backyard.

- **Co-op Research and Extension Services:** The USDA sponsors a nationwide network of agricultural resources through their co-op and extension services. Essentially, it assists local cooperatives—farms, educational institutions, markets, and other cooperative businesses—in research and development related to agriculture and human health. If you live near a Land-Grant institution, you more than likely live near an extension service, which houses local cooperative members in order to assist with disseminating knowledge throughout the community on such topics as sustainable agriculture and food safety and quality. These resources can help you by testing your soil's pH, for example, or providing seminars on organic gardening, or bringing together local gardeners to create a network of support. If you don't have an extension service near you, there are resources online. Check out https://www.usda.gov/topics/rural/cooperative-research-and-extension-services for links.

Third, you must challenge yourself to put words into action: now that you have the tools and resources ready at hand to get started, the next two chapters will guide you through the process of setting up your garden, from preparing the soil and handling seeds to choosing what plants work well together. The great outdoors is calling: let us answer!

CHAPTER 2
Soil And Seeds: Getting Started

The first step to beginning a garden is setting one up in a satisfactory location with a solid foundation; depending on where you live, there are many ways this can be achieved. Then, focus on the soil; this is one of the keys to successful organic gardening, maximizing compost and other organic fertilizers to create a rich and bountiful bed for your vegetables. Once you have your location set up and your soil in place, then you can turn to procuring seeds, nurturing seedlings, and handling transplants.

Foundation: Setting Up Strong

How you set up your garden is most often dictated by where you live. For many of us, the backyard is the best place to set up a garden—though there is a growing movement among some environmentalists to turn all lawn areas into gardens—but you can also successfully garden on a balcony or terrace, even indoors. Light exposure should be one of your first considerations, as most vegetable plants require a certain amount of direct sun during the growing season. With indoor gardening, that can be achieved via a sunny windowsill or, less alluring but workable, with grow lights.

If you plan to set up a garden in the backyard, you must first decide how big your plot will be. I started with a small 8' by 4' plot, just for herbs, chiles, and a couple of tomato plants then expanded with an additional 12' by 4' plot for lettuces, peas, beans, and a variety of other vegetable plants. The size is completely up to you, depending on your yard and your ambition for how much you'd like to grow in the garden. Also remember that, while you can certainly follow some tips for how to maximize space (addressed throughout this book), you also need to be aware not to overcrowd. Staggered planting is the best way to achieve maximum harvest for a small plot: for example, direct seed young lettuces in your garden while you tend to tomato and chile seedlings indoors; once your lettuces are harvested—they will not withstand the heat of summer—transplant your seedlings. Other plants are good for overwintering, such as garlic, when the garden has exhausted its summer heights of production.

Another consideration for setting up your garden is understanding your area's climate or **USDA Plant Hardiness Zone**. There are roughly 11 zones in the United States, which essentially tracks average temperatures throughout the country, with Zone 1 having the coldest average temperatures and Zone 11 having the warmest (click here for a link to the most current USDA map). The zone map does not necessarily track weather patterns other than temperature, however, or note the effects that altitude can have on a growing season. Still, it gives you a rough idea of what plants are most suitable for your area, as well as what times of year one might plant various crops. This is where a resource such as a local garden shop or extension service (see the previous chapter) will come in handy. I have mostly gardened in Zone 7 and have long followed the local wisdom to not plant delicate seedlings before tax day; there's always a chance for an unexpected freeze around Easter Time.

Another issue of note is the quality and kind of soil in your area (obviously, we will discuss how to enhance this below, but nonetheless it is important to note what you're starting with), as well as rainfall averages. This can determine whether you can simply till up a plot of your backyard, add some compost and organic fertilizer, and garden as is. For many if not most places, however, it makes more sense to make a raised bed garden. The raised bed garden has the advantage of allowing water to drain more effectively through the soil—especially if you live in areas where the soil is clay-based—and demarcates a specific area for your garden, not necessarily the backyard. It also means that you more effectively control the quality of soil in which you are cultivating your vegetables; this may be of concern in heavily suburban areas where contamination of the soil by lawn care and other factors—public parks, ponds, golf courses—are of concern. A raised bed also allows for greater distribution of even sunlight.

There are many raised bed options for purchase on the market, some of them raised so far up that the need to bend over is eliminated (though these are for very small-scale operations, for the most part). You can also create your own with a bit of ingenuity and a little extra effort. I like to get untreated, rot-resistant wood planks from a good local source and shingle these together until the bed, once filled with compost and soil, will be about 12" from the subsoil. A quality drill and some rebar can anchor this bed to the ground, with the added benefit that the rebar above the surface allows you to put up some kind of fencing to keep small animals out. Keep the raised bed narrow so that you don't have to walk into the garden, for the most part, and if you put up fencing, cut in a small gate so that you have easy access to the interior when necessary.

Two other concerns for setting up a garden, raised bed or not, are how to get rid of grass, should you be planting in a yarded area, and how to water effectively. To get rid of grass, it is certainly possible to cut out sod and roll it away, though not very practical for the home gardener. What is easier, though not foolproof, is to line your garden bed with cardboard or landscaping fabric before you add your topsoil—though if your concerns are to remain truly organic, be sure to check what these products are made from or treated with. The other effective deterrent to grass is mulch; after planting, keeping a nice layer of organic mulch throughout the garden not only prevents excessive grass growth but also helps to retain moisture and maintain temperature.

When setting up your garden, think carefully about how you intend to water. Installing a drip irrigation system at the beginning of the growing season is highly recommended, though not absolutely necessary. The advantages of drip irrigation, soaker hoses and spot watering emitters, are that it more effectively conserves water than spraying a garden with your hose and that it saves a lot of time throughout the growing season. Another consideration for a watering system is whether or not to use a rain barrel. This collects rainwater, which you can hook up to your hose or irrigation system, for use in watering your garden. It is ecologically sound and efficient, though impractical for areas that get little in the way of rainfall.

Last, consider the pot: if you don't have the space to dig a plot or install a raised bed, you can always garden using pots made of natural or recycled materials. Even if you do have a garden plot in the backyard, pots are an excellent way to grow vegetables and herbs that are sensitive to too much light and heat or have a tendency to take over spaces where they are planted. For example, tender herbs like parsley and chives are sensitive to heat in the height of summer, if they are in pots, they can be moved to shadier areas during the day. And remember that mint—wonderful to use when freshly grown and occurring in a mind-boggling array of varieties (chocolate, lemon, lime, pineapple, to name a few)—will dominate any area in which it is grown. It is always a safer bet to set any mint varietal aside in a pot.

Soil: Food for Plants

Now that you have your garden location set up, the focus turns to the soil, the key to creating a strong and vibrant garden. When gardening organically, the importance of composting cannot be overstated. Not only is it the most successful way to improve and enrich your soil, but it is also environmentally friendly and cost-effective.

Obviously, in your first year of gardening, you must first provide some topsoil, whether from your own backyard or via a garden sourcing outlet. Over time, you may produce enough compost to replenish your soil each year, while adding some organic fertilizers when and if necessary, but at first build a strong foundation. Source your topsoil from a reputable local source or from a garden center that carries organic potting soil. Then, add your compost and get started.

Basically, **composting** is the method by which you break down organic matter—grass, leaves, food waste—into a kind of fertilizer. The goal is to achieve a balance of particular elements that encourage plant growth and, in some cases, discourage pests and disease. Essentially, compositing takes time, some management, and a conscientious view of reusing materials.

Again, there are many varieties of composters on the market, and many are reasonably priced. The advantage to some of these models for purchase is that they can shorten the amount of time it takes to create usable compost. For compost to be useful to your soil, it must have a suitable time and enough internal heat to break down; thus, for first time gardeners who wish to compost in do-it-yourself mode, you must either start composting about a year before you plan to garden (or less with some composting models: check into manufacturer's claims carefully) or buy your compost from a reputable source.

Truly, composting can be virtually cost-free and simple for the do-it-yourself gardener. It simply requires an out of the way space—naturally, composting does give off some odor as it is working and can attract bugs—some basic materials, and patience. I have made my own composting set up using rebar, chicken wire, and dark plastic sheeting: plant the rebar sturdily into the ground in a wide circle (about the size of a backyard garbage can), then wrap it in chicken wire and cover the wire in dark material (recycled plastic works well). The dark covering traps in heat and encourages the aerobic breakdown of the material you put in the composter, while the chicken wire allows for adequate oxygen and moisture levels to penetrate. While not absolutely necessary, a nice covering—I used an untreated round of cedar wood, with a loop of rope for a handle—can speed up the process slightly and keep odor down.

What to put in your composter is simple, but it does require some balance. Lawn cuttings can be put in a composter but beware of overwhelming your compost with cuttings from each mowing throughout the year. Also note whether the grass you are putting in the compost has been treated with petrochemicals, such as fertilizer or herbicides. Leaves raked from the yard near the end of the growing season is an excellent source of compost, but again consider what kind of chemicals the trees in your area may have been treated with. And, of course, food scraps are imperative to creating compost rich in nitrogen: vegetable scraps, fruit peels, coffee grounds (and filters, if organically produced), egg shells, and so on. Avoid meat and dairy products, as these take much longer to break down and can attract a host of unwanted pests.

The ideal is to create a ratio between "green" compost—food scraps, grass clippings, and the like—and "brown" compost—leaves, newspaper, untreated cardboard. Typically, a ratio of 1:3 is ideal (one part green compost to three parts brown compost), but it isn't crucial to be exacting. Basically, green compost heats things up, creating nitrogen and protein, while brown compost adds bulk and carbon to your compost while keeping down the odor. I highly recommend having a kitchen top composter to throw in your scraps while cooking that you can then transfer once or twice a week to your outdoor unit: this convenient setup ensures you keep your composter full and your trash can relatively empty. These units are moderately priced and are available at many garden stores and online.

How does one know when compost is ready? Essentially, it should be broken down by about half, should look like topsoil with few if any individual particles are recognizable, and should have lost any odor other than an earthy soil smell. When mixing in your compost at the beginning of the growing season, take from the bottom up, and leave behind whatever top layer has accumulated in the few months prior. Again, some commercial composters will not require that you take this step.

While compost is the key ingredient to your topsoil, you can also consider other **organic fertilizers**, such as manure and certain meals, to accelerate the health and growth potential of your garden. Manure is the most common addition to gardens, considered a complete fertilizer with lots of organic matter. Never use fresh manure in your garden during the growing season, as this can contaminate plants and lead to illness for anyone consuming them.

Organic bone meal and blood meal can also be used to assist your soil's potential: bone meal contains calcium and phosphate and promotes strong root health, while blood meal is high in nitrogen and stimulates leaf growth (though too much can burn plant roots, so apply judiciously). There are also fish and seaweed-based meals and emulsions for the garden. I can attest personally to the efficacy of fish skeletons: after a particularly successful fishing season, I will keep my fish scraps, frozen, until the end of growing season then simply till them into the soil before overwintering (even throwing in some past-their-prime whole carcasses). This technique has led to some of my lushest gardens.

Last, one option to consider when starting an organic garden is to get your **soil tested**. Finding out the pH of your soil can help you determine what kinds of organic fertilizers and how much compost to add. This can be done at an extension center (see Chapter 1) or at some local gardening centers; home testing kits are also increasingly available. What this test will tell you is how acidic or alkaline your soil is: most plants prefer a soil that is very slightly acidic with a pH of about 6.5 (7 is considered neutral). This is the level at which the most important nutrients, including nitrogen and potassium, are most available to plants. Usually, lime is used to treat acidic soils, while sulfur is used to treat alkaline soils. This is where an extension center becomes very useful, as their testing can pinpoint exactly what nutrients your soil lacks and/or what nutrients are too prominent. Thus, you can amend your soil with more or less of whatever specific nutrient you may need, different plants requiring different amounts, an issue that will be discussed in the next chapter.

Seeds: Nurturing Success

There are many venues from which to procure seeds, such as via seed catalogs, local farms, and seed saving. Remember that, when attempting to garden organically, the seeds themselves must come from an organic source; this does not mean that hybrids cannot be used, but it does bar the use of genetically modified seeds. Thankfully, GMO seeds are not much of a problem for the home gardener, as they are typically relegated to large industrial crops, such as corn and canola, but it does not hurt to check. Some tomato varieties—the Flavr Savr, for example—are indeed GMO products, and the FDA has recently approved GMO potatoes for market.

But, for the home gardener, the biggest decision will be whether to use heirloom varieties—which are older varieties passed down through generations—or hybridized seeds. Heirloom varieties are wonderful and can expand our experience of what certain vegetables taste like, though they can be hard to grow if they are not originally local to your area. Hybridized varieties are typically hardier but can be less impressive than heirlooms. For the first time gardener, I would recommend sourcing some of both, to ensure maximum harvest while providing a valuable learning experience.

To clarify, the difference between GMO seeds and hybridized seeds is that one is a high-tech, relatively new innovation in creating almost entirely new plants while the other is a centuries-old tradition of selective cross-breeding of similar plants to produce a heartier version.

Hybridized seeds cross different strains of the same plant to maximize the best qualities of each strain. Thus, a hybridized plant may come from two strains, one that proved to be particularly abundant and one that proved particularly disease-resistant; the hybridized plant created from this mix thrives well and survives well. Hybrids have been nurtured to match human desires for centuries: the corn that we recognize today is the result of thousands of years of hybridization, selecting for the plant that produced the largest ears; corn is a grass plant, and early corn produced tiny, tough, inedible-without-processing kernels. Through crossing strains over time, we now have large ears of corn with juicy, ready-to-eat kernels. The disadvantage to using hybridized seeds is that they do not necessarily reproduce in exactly the same manner each season; that is, if you save seeds from a hybridized plant to use the following season, these may or may not produce the desired qualities initially derived from the hybrid plant. So, buying seeds each year, while not necessary, is recommended to achieve the same results in a hybridized strain.

GMO seeds have been genetically engineered in a laboratory, produced quickly by technological means and not subject to years of selective breeding. Since these kinds of seeds have only been widely used since the early 90s, there is still little known about the environmental consequence of adding these seeds and plants to the biome. GMO seeds are not limited to cross-breeding within their plant family, and thus, science has produced seeds that are genetically engineered to contain bacteria and, in some cases, viruses, along with the original plant matter. While advocates of GMO products point to their success in creating a more stable food supply enabling food security for more people, critics are quick to point out that the unintended consequences of such genetic engineering have yet to be measured, in terms of environmental stability and human health. Stories abound of third world countries rejecting genetically modified products (research "Golden Rice" for an example) as an extension of colonial domination, relegating local populations to the status of unwitting guinea pigs. While the European Union has more closely monitored the use of GMOs in its food supply than the United States, the National Organic Program has designated the use of GMOs in organically labeled food unacceptable.

The other type of seed to consider when raising an organic garden at home is the **heirloom seed**: these are traditional seed varieties that have passed down throughout generations with little to no manipulation. Most heirloom plants are raised from seeds that have been around for 50 years or longer. Considered the pinnacle of organic gardening, heirloom seeds are excitingly refreshing, diverse, and somewhat challenging to grow. When choosing heirloom seeds, be sure to look for varietals that have been commonly cultivated in your area; this means they will be prepared for the climate of said area and have some natural defenses against the local pests and diseases, usually. For example, Cherokee Purple tomatoes grow well in my area, though I've heard that they are difficult to grow farther north. These open-pollinators are the best plants to use if you are considering saving seeds for the next garden season.

Some popular **seed catalogs** *to pursue include Seed Savers Exchange, Eden Brothers Heirloom Seeds, Johnny's Selected Seeds, Southern Exposure Seed Exchange, and the ubiquitous Burpee Seeds (which includes a section on heirlooms).*

Once you start your garden, **seed saving** is an incredibly cost-effective and environmentally sound practice to replenish your garden for the following year. There are many places where you can order seed saving kits, but it is a practice that's simple enough to follow at home with a handful of old, empty spice jars, or paper envelopes. Make sure your seeds are dry and free of debris before tucking them away for next season in a cool, dry place. The Seed Savers Exchange site contains lots of useful information on how to save seeds, as well as advice on which seeds are most practical for the typical home gardener to save (some plants require more effort than others to grow from saved seeds; reliable ones to save include bean and tomato seeds).

Now that you have your seeds, the decision as to how best to use them—direct seeding or seeding and transplanting—depends on what you are growing and where. For the home gardener, it is often most practical to utilize a mix of direct seeding and transplanting, either via purchasing seedlings or fostering them at home. It takes a dedicated gardener to put in the time and effort required to start seedlings from scratch and transplant later in the season, so be aware of how much time you are willing to spend. Many seeds can and should be sown directly into the garden and, while technically speaking, one can grow any plant from a seed in the soil, in many cases using seedlings makes better sense for the home gardener.

Direct seeding is when you sow the seeds directly into your prepared garden soil. This technique is great for delicate plants that don't take well to transplanting, like lettuces and greens. Usually, seed packets will have instructions on how deep to plant and how far apart to place seeds and certainly follow those. But don't worry too terribly much about spacing when it comes to the tiny lettuce seeds; it is inevitable that you'll accidentally drop more than one seed right next to each other in your shallow row. Simply start separating plants, thinning your lettuce patch, once they've grown to height large enough to harvest some bay leaves. Be sure to pull the plant up by its roots to leave its neighbor enough room to grow. Enjoy the baby lettuces immediately and compost the roots. With many lettuce and greens varietals (kale, collards, swiss chard), you can cut leaves to use, leaving roots in ground so leaves grow back, at least two or three times before the lettuce will start to taste too strong or bitter. At that point, simply pull up the roots and compost or, if you have the room, leave them to go to seed should you have the patience to try to harvest the minute seeds.

Direct seeding is also appropriate for plants with climbing vines, such as sugar snap peas and pole beans. Seed these next to your fence and encourage vines to grow into the mesh or wires. Beware of vines snaking into other parts of your garden, however; you might create an internal barrier, as well, to keep the vines in their place.

Tomatoes, of course, are technically vines, though most have sturdier "trunks" and grow like haphazard bushes. The best way to tame a tomato plant is to put a circular tomato cage around it when the plant gets a foot or so off the ground. Otherwise, you'll end up with tomato vines lying on the ground, which causes the fruit to rot or leaves it unripe without direct sunlight.

The other factor when determining whether to direct seed or use **transplants** is the climate. Some plants will survive a hard freeze—indeed, many need it to grow successfully—but many will not. Thus, seedlings that are nurtured in greenhouses or indoors are excellent shortcuts to getting a jump on the growing season, particularly if you live in colder climes, and a convenient way to plan your garden space with a clear visual representation of what will be sprouting up where.

Experience has led me to direct seed lettuces, greens, and beans and to use transplanted seedlings for tomatoes, chiles, and herbs, just as a few examples. Root vegetables, of course, are difficult to transplant without disturbing or destroying the edible root itself. In the next chapter, some specific vegetables and herbs well-suited for the organic home garden are discussed in detail, with some advice on how to treat each.

CHAPTER 3
Vegetable Victory: Choosing the Best Plants for Your Garden

In addition to determining which plants you'll grow, this chapter should help you with how to maximize the space in your garden and how to utilize companion planting. This is the time-honored idea that certain plants grown together nurture each other by attracting beneficial insects and repelling pests while also providing each other with nutrients and/or other kinds of support.

Before jumping into the following list (and to fend off endless arguments around the dinner table), I am indeed characterizing some plants that are technically fruits—tomatoes, cucumbers, chiles—as suitable for a vegetable garden, as well as including herbs. I think even the most hidebound gardening expert will agree that any home garden worth its salt will include some, if not all, of these interlopers.

Last, this list provides a very general overview of each plant. When and how to plant will depend on what zone you live in and what kind of garden you have decided to cultivate. Some basic tips are provided; consult with local sources for details about how to get each and every plant you choose to thrive in your organic garden. See Chapter 5 for ideas on how to use your plants in the kitchen.

Herbs:

Among the easiest and arguably some of the most useful plants to cultivate in your garden, herbs are nearly as indispensable to the home cook as salt and pepper. Additionally, herbs can be readily grown in pots, leaving the bulk of your raised bed to other plants (if using a drip irrigation system, pots are fairly easy to integrate with spot watering emitters). It is undeniably satisfying to simply pop outside and scissor off a small handful of herbs to enhance any meal during the growing season. And many herbs will return each year—again, depending on your location—and be some of the first pleasures to be harvested at the start of the next spring.

Herbs can be either direct seeded or grown from seed and transplanted into your garden if you like, though herb seeds are typically so tiny that they are difficult to handle. I prefer to procure seedlings from a reliable local source who uses organic methods. With annual herbs, plant seedlings after the last frost.

Parsley

Truly, one of the invaluable workhorses of the garden—and the kitchen—parsley is more than just a garnish; it can be a major player in salads and fresh sauces. Italian flat-leaf parsley is my go-to; it is more robust in flavor than curly parsley and its broad, flat leaves are more appealing in many applications. Parsley can stand the full sun, though it isn't as hearty as basil. If you live in a hot climate, plant in a pot that can be moved to shaded areas when the weather gets really warm. Takes about two to three months to mature. If your area does not get terribly cold winters, parsley may come back, but only for another year.

Basil

Another garden wonder, Genovese basil is a marvelously hearty, generous plant that reaches about two feet in height at full maturity. I have also grown globe basil and purple (Thai) basil; all are good, though Genovese is the most "all-purpose" varietal. Plant in the garden bed for best results. There are many other heirloom varieties of basil, though Genovese is one of the strongest and most productive kinds you can grow. It takes about three months to reach its full potential but can be carefully clipped throughout the season. Basil likes full sun—and does NOT like cold at all, so don't clip and store in the refrigerator, as it will wilt and turn black quickly—and trim back the flowers that appear during the season to keep your plant from bolting. A lot of instructions will say "pinch" off flowers, but the rough action of pinching can allow for greater disease penetration into the plant. Cutting is always healthier.

Chives

One of the earliest harbingers of spring, chives will keep cropping up for several years before they need replanting. As such, I keep chives in pots so that when I am ready to till my garden plot for the new spring season, I don't worry about digging up the chives. Don't limit yourself only to delicate "onion-y" chives; the stronger flavor of garlic chives is marvelous in a lot of Asian cooking and otherwise. Chives thrive in most zones and require very little attention to do well. When they flower, don't make the mistake of getting rid of the chive blossoms; they are a delicious garnish, or, if you end up with a lot of them, soak them in vinegar for a few days to make a flavored vinegar for salad dressings.

Mint

Virtually indestructible, I have grown numerous varieties of mint over the years—spearmint, peppermint, lime mint, chocolate mint, Corsican mint—and have only managed to sabotage a plant one time by attempting to plant it in a frustratingly wet part of the yard. Even mint couldn't withstand the onslaught of water. As cautioned before, mint will quite easily take over a garden, so segregate your mint plants in pots. Along with chives, mint will be one of the first plants to pop up in early spring. It will return for several years, as well, and like basil, mint does not enjoy being put in the 'fridge. If you clip a little more than you wanted, put the rest in a water glass with a bit of water and leave on the countertop for a day or two.

Tarragon

An underutilized herb in American cooking, tarragon has a lovely and delicate anise-like flavor. It is wonderful to stuff a chicken with, along with lemon and garlic, as well as to roast, and making tarragon vinegar is an end of season treat around my house. Tarragon likes full sun, as well, making it a good choice for planting in the garden. It grows close to the ground and likes to spread out, so give it some room to do so. This is an herb that takes well to drying, unlike basil and chives, so be sure to rescue it before winter sets in.

Oregano

Absolutely essentially for Italian and Mexican cooking, I always have oregano on hand. It is impossible to buy fresh or dried oregano that is equal to what you can grow in your own garden (though, arguably, that could be said of most herbs). This is another low growing plant and, while it does not need as much room as tarragon, give it a good 10" of space to flourish in. Along with basil and tarragon, plant this one in your bed. Because it hugs the ground, it can be susceptible to overwatering.

Other Herbs

There are many other herbs that I have grown organically with great success; the above are merely the ones I prefer to always have on hand. If you like dill, it is a natural pest repellent, so it is a great fit for your garden bed. Don't forget cilantro (which I don't plant but love: there's only so much space in the garden, and cilantro is cheap at my local market), of course. Sage, rosemary, and thyme are all great candidates for drying at the end of the season. There are also less common herbs, such as lemon verbena (delicious though aggressive in the garden like mint), lavender (as pretty as it is fragrant), and lovage (a celery-flavored herb).

Vegetables:

The crowning achievement of any home garden, and the envy of every neighbor, will certainly be the beautiful crop of multicolored, delicious, and nutritious vegetables that you coax out of your lovingly tended soil. The following are merely a handful of suggestions, included because they thrive well in organic gardens and are, for the most part, relatively easy to tend. I also tried to include representative vegetables for each season, so that you can practice succession planting, if you like, ensuring a continuous crop of homegrown, organic produce throughout the year. See Chapter 7 for more on the practice of succession planting.

Lettuces

Direct seed in early spring for lovely tender greens throughout spring and early summer. Most lettuces do not like intense heat, so give your garden space to other plants for summer. At the onset of fall, as your summer crops start to fade, replant lettuces for a later harvest. As mentioned in the previous chapter, don't worry too much about placing a single seed in a single hole with lettuce; simply carve out a shallow trough and sprinkle seeds down the length of it. Thin your crop as necessary once they start leafing out; use the baby lettuces in early spring salads. Crisphead types of lettuce tend to be the heartiest and less vulnerable to pests, so these are good for the first-time gardener. But do be adventurous and try looseleaf, butterhead, and romaine varietals, too. Most lettuces will produce at least two nice heads, sometimes three: cut the leaves near the base of the plant instead of pulling up by the roots to get a second or third harvest.

Greens

Other green plants that love the springtime are spinach, arugula, swiss chard, and various Asian greens (mizuna, gai lan, bok choy). Direct seed in early spring and, like lettuce, these greens will continue to produce until the heat of summer sets in. These plants can also be cultivated in early fall, though I like to switch to hearty kale and collard greens at that time of year, along with savoyed spinach which can produce through much of the winter, as well. All of these greens produce well in cooler weather, but need direct sunlight and adequate water. Be advised: insects enjoy munching on lettuce and leafy greens as much as we do. Just expect to lose a bit to the bugs. See Chapter 4 for more on combating pests.

Sugar Snap Peas

I gardened for many years before I took a chance on sugar snap peas (and pole beans), thinking that these would be too much trouble, with their vine-y needs. Turns out, they're easy to grow (especially if you've had experience with the wily ways of tomato plants) and find their way onto whatever trellis you set up for them. Direct seed in early spring in the corner of your garden, where you've cordoned off a portion (say, about 2' in from your garden's border) with some chicken wire or recycled plastic fencing. The pea tendrils need something to grab onto, and this keeps them from latching on to other plants. These are among the first vegetables to mature in the spring. Other peas, such as English peas or snow peas, can also be grown this way; I simply like the ease—no shelling!—and taste of the sugar snap. Once sugar snaps are done, pole beans start producing.

Radishes

Another early spring crop, radishes are quick growing, taking only about a month to mature. Direct seed in the garden (as with root vegetables, transplanting does not work well). Depending on your climate, you can produce two or three rounds of radishes before the weather gets too warm. Radishes thrive in weather that does not get much above 70 degrees. Keep soil moist for best results. French breakfast radishes are a favorite of mine, tender and mild, and Easter egg radishes produce lovely pink, purple, and red bouquets.

Cruciferous Vegetables

Cabbage, broccoli, cauliflower, and Brussel sprouts are the most common cruciferous vegetables seen in markets and gardens. Of these, broccoli and cabbage are easier to grow, while cauliflower is the most temperamental. As with lettuces and greens, these are early spring and fall crops (Brussel sprouts are the last to harvest at the end of the fall). To make a harvest worth your while, you must have enough room in your garden plot to grow a nice row or two. These are also best when direct seeded.

Pole Beans

These are the easiest kind of beans to grow, akin to peas (see above for more details on where to plant). They need a trellis and some time, and you'll have a satisfying harvest. Since these harvest later in the season, you can—if pressed for space—direct sow these after your sugar snaps are done for the season in early summer; your trellis will already be in place and ready for climbing. If your climate gets terribly hot early in summer, the beans may not produce much, however. I like Provider beans, in particular; they are a prolific producer. Harvest often to encourage more growth. Note: growing beans to dry is a different matter entirely, and one that is beyond the spatial confines of most home gardeners.

Okra

This plant is extremely prolific and does very well in hot, humid climates, though it can be grown almost anywhere that it can get direct sunlight. Transplant in late spring and grow only as many plants as you think you will use; in my area, gardeners are hard-pressed to give it away at the height of summer, so much okra is growing. Also, be sure to monitor the plants well once they start producing. Okra is at its tastiest when it is about the length of a pinky finger, and within the space of a day, it can nearly double in size.

Tomatoes

These guys are the reason I started gardening in the first place: compare a homegrown tomato to a supermarket tomato and you will instantly see why. While all produce tastes better coming out of the ground, fresh and organically grown, tomatoes in particular showcase the glories of home gardening (and the horrors of what industrial agriculture has done to this beloved fruit). There are so many varieties of tomatoes out there that a type of tomato that can be grown in virtually any location. These plants can be direct seeded indoors in late winter/early spring for transplanting after the last frost. Typically, I don't risk planting seedlings until after tax day in my Zone 7 area. Caring for seedlings indoors is time-consuming, but cost effective if you plan on growing lots of tomato plants. I like to get my seedlings locally from an organic producer, as I only grow about six or seven plants each season.

Tomatoes need direct sun and adequate water throughout the growing season. In my garden, tomatoes start producing in earnest in July (I usually get lucky with a couple at the end of June) and continue through October, excepting drought years with 100+ degree temperatures. Once seedlings are planted and start thriving, put up a tomato cage around each plant. Give your tomato plants plenty of room to flourish, and check on them regularly once they start growing fast and producing, gently taming the vines through the cage. Tomato vines will always start to look a bit wild at the height of the growing season, so don't worry too much about that, as long as they are healthy. Also, beware of the avian risks from above: the first year I planted tomato seedlings, I left them alone for a couple of hours to make dinner. When I went to check on them that evening, the birds had stripped all the leaves off every single plant! Most survived, but since then, I've strung a makeshift net over the perimeter of the garden—make sure netting is suspended so as not to smother the plants—to prevent such an apocalypse. Just about everyone, birds and bugs and marauding neighborhood children, love tomatoes: see Chapter 4 for some help with all but the neighborhood kids.

I like to grow cherry or grape tomatoes (Black Cherry and Yellow Pear are favorites) in a large pot near the garden, as these smaller plants don't need as much room and often don't require cages. They also mature faster and are ready to pluck off the vine and throw into a salad in mid-summer. For other varieties, I tend to rely on heirloom tomatoes that are local to my area, such as Arkansas Travelers, Cherokee Purples, and Royal Hillbilly tomatoes (a rarer heirloom most definitely worth seeking out); check with your local farmers' market or gardening store for what varietals might be common for your location. Other famous heirlooms include Brandywine and Green Zebra (this one remains green when ripe). If you are interested in canning, paste tomatoes work best for this, the San Marzano being the standard-bearer. Be sure to visit Chapters 5 and 6 for many suggestions on how to use and preserve these beauties.

Cucumbers

Another prolific, vine-y plant, cucumbers thrive in most warm climates. Since they are so prolific, and since their vines tend to grow willy-nilly, I recommend setting up another small bed for them (which can also be used for larger squash varieties and/or melons) or, at the least, cordoning off a section of the garden to limit the vine expansion within the rest of your bed. There are numerous varieties of cucumbers you can grow, from traditional slicing and pickling cucumbers to Asian types that have fewer seeds. I did not bother with cucumbers for a long time—they are cheap and plentiful in the supermarket, albeit grown industrially and most often coated with wax—until I discovered the Armenian cucumber: these pale varietals produce large, long fruit with small seed pods and a clean, crisp taste that reminds you that cucumbers are closely related to melons. They produce so well (and don't turn bitter even when large) that I supplied a local restaurant for a couple of years from my small patch. One decent sized Armenian cucumber can provide a side dish for a table of six or eight people. Direct seed in the garden in spring in a plot that gets lots of direct sunshine; most cucumber varieties thrive throughout the hot summer into early fall.

A quick tip: if you grow cucumbers (or tomatoes or melons) and you have any issues with sensitive skin, I'd recommend wearing long sleeves or long gloves when weeding and harvesting among these vines. Cucumber vines will make me itch for two days if I don't cover my skin when rooting through them.

Melons

Another low-growing vine, melons can be prolific given enough space and by choosing the right varietal for your climate. For most backyard gardeners, the familiar melon crops of watermelon, honeydew, and cantaloupe are not practical to grow because of space issues. If you would like to grow some—and growing melons organically produces beautiful, pure-tasting fruit (essentially, a melon is a water filtration system)—investigate some lesser known, smaller varieties such as Chanterais melons. When mature, they fit in the palm of your hand and have the flavor of a sweeter cantaloupe. They aren't as easy to grow everywhere—too much or too little water will hamper their development—but with some nurturing, these are tasty treats to harvest throughout the summer. Treat like cucumbers (above) when planting.

Chile & Other Peppers

Chile and bell peppers are colorful and tasty additions to your garden. They are also, for the most part, quite hearty and produce well in warm regions. The larger the pepper, the more room it will need, of course; otherwise, most pepper varieties can be planted in spring for a harvest throughout the summer and into early fall. I have had success with typical peppers like jalapenos, serranos, Anaheims, and poblanos. I've also grown padrons, lovely Spanish peppers that can be sautéed in olive oil and eaten whole (the fun is in the surprise: most are sweet and mild, but one or two will pack a spicy punch); shishitos, a Japanese pepper treated similarly to padrons; habaneros, the super spicy brilliant orange pepper; Bolivian rainbow peppers, more of an ornamental plant with its purple, red, and orange bouquets of small peppers; and huge bushes of cayennes, which I use to make pretty *ristras* (the pepper wreaths you find in the Southwest) for drying. Grinding your own cayenne powder will ruin you for the dusty supermarket stuff forever. Most peppers are easy to grow—IF you have a decently long summer.

Squash & the Like

Squash, like okra, can be an over-performer in warm climates, though their easygoing presence ensures likely garden success. Again, squash varieties need space to spread out and flourish, so make sure you have adequate room. Direct seed in spring for a late summer abundance. Try zucchini, yellow crook-necked squash, and patty pan varietals which do well in most regions with a stretch of summer.

Other squash varieties, such as acorn and butternut, mature later and grow larger. Thus they are good for fall harvesting. However, they need more space and time accordingly. Also, eggplant, which is technically a nightshade plant, is similar in its growing capacity and timing as squash.

Alliums (Garlic & Onions & Leeks)

Garlic and onions are excellent crops to grow in a small garden if you follow succession planting: these are typically overwintered; thus, you plant in late fall for a harvest the next spring or early summer, clearing out that space for later plantings at the height of the growing season. There are many places to source garlic and onion bulbs, and you will be surprised at the amazing variety that is available: Filaree Garlic Farms has an outstanding collection of organic, heirloom bulb varieties from which to choose, and I've successfully grown more than a dozen different kinds of garlic and shallots (Filaree Farms also has a selection of potato seeds and other plants). If you aren't interested in exotic varietals, you can literally just buy a head of garlic in the store and plant the bulbs in your garden, root end down. Thrifty, if not guaranteed heirloom. In my area, I plant in mid- to late October and harvest in early June. Usually, I plant 50 or 60 bulbs because garlic—like onions and shallots—will keep if stored properly until your next growing season.

Leeks grow in both spring and fall, so you can plant seeds in late summer (after you've harvested your garlic and shallots, say) to mature over fall and winter. Pluck them in spring to be replaced by your spring seedlings. The allium family is an excellent source for creating a year-round garden experience.

Potatoes

This is another crop that needs a lot of room to make it worth your while, but if you have it, the sheer variety of potatoes available along with their long shelf life creates an exciting crop. Potatoes do best in cool soil, so be sure to time your planting so that harvesting can be done before the heat of summer settles in. Some varieties take well to overwintering, while others can be planted in the early spring to harvest at the beginning of summer. My grandparents grew potatoes by cutting out the eyes of older, withered potatoes and planting them; for more certain results, source some seed potatoes from a reputable grower (Filaree Garlic Farms or Seed Savers Exchange are reliable online sources).

Some Less Common Considerations

All of the above-mentioned crops are good candidates for organic gardening and allow you to stagger your planting throughout the year in order to make the best use of your garden space. There are many, many other vegetables and fruits out there for consideration, as well. The above are crops with which I have familiarity growing and, for the most part, are relatively easy to grow. Some other crops I adore, like asparagus and berries of all kinds, I seek out at farmers' markets rather than grow myself, simply because they are either temperamental or so delicious to pests that I can't keep up with them. Another crop I have tried and failed to grow—it is just too warm where I am—is artichokes; there are some excellent heirloom varieties out there just waiting for you to discover.

In addition, the world of gardening is whatever you make of it. You are limited only by location, and even then, you can sometimes exercise some control over nature via a greenhouse or hoop house planting. I have indulged in the rather more time consuming practice some seasons of moving plants from outdoors to indoors to outdoors: a small kumquat tree that thrived for several years by protecting it from winter; a bay leaf tree that produces a continuous supply of leaves (fresh bay leaves are astoundingly fragrant); and many ornamental plants, some I've had for more than a decade. Gardening in any form is a kind of rare pleasure in our technologically saturated age. Take a chance and get your hands dirty—in a good way!

Companion Planting:

This is the practice of planting certain groups of plants together in order to gain from their mutually beneficial characteristics. These characteristics include complimentary nutrient needs, abilities to repel pests, and/or habits of growth. Companion planting has long been used in many cultures, the received wisdom of hundreds of generations of farmers who have learned, through trial and error, what works well together.

Before the onslaught of industrial agriculture, companion planting was a reliable way in which farmers could ensure decent harvests. For one example, think of Native American cultures, where the planting of maize (corn), beans, and squash is ubiquitous: the tall maize plants shade the low-growing squash while providing a natural trellis for the climbing beans; in turn, the prickly vines of the squash discourage pests, and the nitrogen-rich beans provide soil nutrients. Some version of this ancient wisdom can be employed in any backyard plot.

- **Herbs** are excellent natural pest repellants: for example, strong scented herbs such as basil and dill are fine companions for tomatoes, warding off hornworms. Rosemary, sage, and mint can keep moths that munch on greens at bay. Other herbs attract beneficial insects, such as ladybugs that eat leaf-destroying aphids (parsley is good for this). Many gardeners swear by marigolds which act to protect roots, fending off harmful worms. Earthworms are great garden companions, but there a host of nematodes out there that will thrive on your plant roots rather than your soil.

- **Shade** is crucial to certain plants: leafy greens like a bit of shade if you want them to last into late spring or early summer, so taller plants can act as a shield against the sun.

- **Space** can also be a common sense product of companion planting wisdom: planting lower growing herbs such as tarragon, oregano, and rosemary in between tomato plants give vines room to spread while also providing pest protection. Also, sequential planting is another sub-category of companion planting—planting continuously throughout the year (see above for examples)—has the added benefit of discouraging weed growth.

- **Nutrient** swapping benefits various companion plants while also boosting the quality of your soil. For example, nitrogen-rich plants such as peas or beans (or cover crops:

see Chapter 7) replenish your soil of the nitrogen that is much needed by tomatoes.

- **Seasonality** is a basic rule of thumb when considering companion planting: for example, radishes and greens grow well together, as they both like cool temperatures and well-drained soil; tomatoes and squash grow well together, as they both like lots of sun and do well in heat, while peppers also thrive at this time of year and provide some natural pest repellent.

These are merely a handful of examples of the vast reserve of material concerning the benefits and techniques of companion planting. Farmers Almanacs, farmers' markets, cooperative extension services are all excellent places to get further advice on how to set up your garden for maximum success.

CHAPTER 4
Preparing for Pests: Embrace the Inevitable

The first rule of organic gardening that I learned after going to a seminar at the local cooperative extension service was simple: "one for me, one for the pests." It can be frustrating when you start gardening organically, especially if heretofore you have used traditional petrochemical fertilizers (MiracleGro) and pesticides (Sevin Dust) as quick fixes. Indeed, it can be heartbreaking to find a gnawed leaf or a wormy tomato after all the time and effort invested in creating your lovely garden.

However, I would strongly argue that the quick fix benefits of petrochemical fertilizers and pesticides are absolutely not worth it in the long term: the effects on the health of your soil, the potential contamination of groundwater, the ethical conundrum of sourcing petroleum-based products, not to mention the proven health risks posed to humans, far outweigh the perceived benefit of producing more unblemished produce.

Besides, organic gardening also attracts welcome critters, such as ladybugs and earthworms, while the use of petrochemicals indiscriminately lays waste to your microbiome. Accepting the inevitable does not mean that you accept defeat; in fact, it means that you embrace the thriving biological community that you have worked diligently to foster and nurture. That said, we'd all still like to put more of our produce on our own plates rather than leave them to the pests. See below for some ideas on how to manage your potential pest population.

Note: I don't bother to address herbicides as they really should have no place in a backyard garden. Fertilizer is dealt with in Chapter 2.

Organic Pesticides

There are many quality organic pesticides on the market currently, as demand for purer products has continued to gain prominence in the last twenty years. If you decide to invest in buying these products commercially, look for the OMRI seal: this indicates that the product has been vetted by the Organic Materials Review

Institute, a non-profit organization that works under the auspices of the NOP (USDA's National Organic Program). This seal should give you confidence that the product meets the highest standards as designated by the government.

If, however, you wish to circumvent the use of commercial products, then there are any number of pesticides that you can make at home, with some easy-to-source ingredients. Stock up on some spray bottles for ease of use.

- **Neem oil** has been used for centuries by native farmers for its overall effectiveness at keeping pests away. The juice from the neem plant has been shown to contain fifty or more natural pesticides. Organic neem oil can be found at many garden stores and online. Mix half an ounce into two quarts of warm water with about a teaspoon of organic liquid soap. It loses effectiveness as it sits so use within a day or two.

- **Mineral oil** is also an effective pesticide, in that it dehydrates insect eggs. Mix about twenty milliliters of quality mineral oil into a liter of warm water.

- **Citrus oil** mixed with cayenne pepper is particularly effective on ants. Essential citrus oil can be found in many natural food stores and online. Mix a few drops of essential oil (about ten) into a cup of warm water, then stir in a teaspoon of cayenne. Use immediately. Another use for citrus oil is to mix a full ounce of orange essential oil along with three tablespoons of organic liquid soap into a gallon of water. This seems to work well on slugs.

- **Eucalyptus oil** wards off wasps and flies (though it also deters bees, which you might want around). Simply sprinkle a few drops around where you've seen the wasps or flies, and the strong scent will keep them away.

- **Salt spray** is an incredibly simple and effective way to get rid of spider mites. Mix a couple of tablespoons of coarse salt (some recommend Himalayan salt in particular) into a gallon of water, then spray directly onto affected plants.

- **Garlic and onion spray** is a longer lasting solution that will keep for a couple of weeks, refrigerated. Chop a clove or two of organic garlic and a medium-sized organic onion and add to a quart of warm water. Let sit for an hour or two, then add a teaspoon of cayenne and a tablespoon of organic liquid soap. Strain out solids before putting into a spray bottle, but keep solids in any solution that you store.

- **Some other suggestions** are to make a tea from chrysanthemum flowers, dropping in some neem oil to enhance effectiveness; or to make a tobacco spray by steeping loose tobacco in warm water overnight; or to mix chile powder with diatomaceous earth and water. These are mentioned with reservations as the first two can actually be harmful to certain plants and the latter can weigh down delicate plants.

Other Home Remedies

Organic gardeners learn quickly how to get creative in the battle against pests. The above organic recipes for pesticides are a surefire start, but there are other tricks and tips that gardeners pass along, word of mouth, to help with certain problems. (Remember: insects aren't the only creatures who might find your garden attractive.) The efficacy of the following methods has not been put to rigorous scientific testing; nevertheless, many of them are simple, common sense ideas that are easily employed and arguably effective.

- **Coffee grounds and eggshells** sprinkled around the base of a tomato plant will keep hornworms from crawling across that prickly barrier and up to your vines and fruits. Other gardeners swear by planting an old coffee can with the bottom cut out to encircle your seedling; this does work but can impede root growth.

- **Beer** can also be used to attract certain critters like slugs. Bury a container of beer in the ground near your plants (alternatively, place a low saucer next to them); the bugs will crawl in but not emerge.

- **Diatomaceous earth** is a natural substance composed of finely ground fossilized material and works much like eggshells and coffee grounds. As with the aforementioned, this should be sprinkled only around affected plants so as not to disturb your soil's balance.

- **Hand picking** slugs, snails, and hornworms off your plants is a low-tech, non-intrusive way to get rid of these pests, should they make it to your plants. Drop the intruders into a bucket of brine to kill them. Do this in the early morning when the slugs are active for best results.

- **Vinegar** can be easily used to keep away small pests, especially fruit flies (which actually should more appropriately be called "vinegar" flies, as they are attracted to the gases that fruits release—which is mimicked by vinegar—not the fruit itself). For outdoor use, spray lightly on pest areas; this can also be used on weeds, but be careful not to harm your own plants. For indoor use, put vinegar in a small bowl next to your problem area—produce that isn't refrigerated or next to an indoor composter—and cover with plastic wrap punctured with toothpick-sized holes.

- **Netting** is almost indispensable if you live in an area that attracts any number of critters, from rabbits and possums to birds and neighborhood cats. Netting can sometimes be a nuisance—and can ensnare butterflies—but usually it is worth saving the garden from the raiding hordes. Even **cheesecloth** can be used, draped over plants; it allows for light and water to penetrate, but its fine holes will keep out small pests and insects. It isn't as durable as garden netting.

- **Foil strips** can also be used, scarecrow-like, to keep birds away. Change locations regularly to ensure you keep them on their toes.

- **Fake snakes** have been an effective deterrent to rabbits and birds for me in the past. Again, change their location regularly.

- **Mulch** is an effective way to keep your soil moist and regulate temperature. Cedar and eucalyptus mulch are also reported to be good at keeping pests away, as the strong scents repel many insects. Mulch also works to keep weeds down during the growing season. You can use a mulch to protect your soil over the winter if you aren't succession planting or using cover crops.

Combating Disease

I have found that disease has been more destructive to my gardens than pests and that many diseases come down to soil health and simple maintenance techniques. The best way to combat disease is to prevent it, and there are several simple things that you can do to avoid common garden problems.

- **Soil health** is perhaps the most important step to preventing disease. See Chapter 2 for more details on how to prepare your soil, but as a reminder, one of the best things you can do before the main gardening season begins (or, indeed, at the end, so you can get a jump on next year's plans) is to have your soil tested. Be sure that the pH is at the right level (for most edible plants, that pH is around 6.5), and that your soil nutrients are at sufficient levels. Too little nitrogen in your soil prohibits or stunts growth, while too little calcium can cause the dreaded bottom end rot in tomatoes. Regular testing and correcting of your soil can head off a multitude of problems.

- **Proper maintenance** is also simple but key. Over-fertilizing a garden can foster disease so use a judicious hand. Keep your equipment clean and get rid of old rusty tools, especially pruners, and do use tools rather than pinching or tearing for pruning work. The more ragged you leave the stem when pruning or bobbing flowering shoots, the more vulnerable the plant is to disease. Perhaps most important, **water in the morning** so that plants have time to dry before nightfall; this prevents fungal diseases, among the most prominent problems for home gardens. In the event of an exceptionally wet spring, do keep a careful eye out for fungal diseases like tomato blight. If not tackled immediately, this will stunt and eventually kill your tomato plant.

- **Natural fungicides** such as bicarbonates can be used preventatively to avoid blight, rot, and mildew. Baking soda can be used though it isn't nearly as effective as bicarbonates containing ammonium or potassium. These are considered non-toxic to humans. GreenCure is a well-regarded fungicide readily available on the market.

- **Biological fungicides** such as Bacillus subtilis are effective in combating many common diseases in the garden with no harmful effects to humans or animals. While prevention is still better, the biological fungicides can be helpful in combating disease once it has already spread.

- **Copper and sulfur-based products** can be used for prevention, as well, though they can sometimes be harmful to certain plants and animals. So, these should be used with caution.

- **Soil bacteria-based products** are used to protect roots and seeds while causing no harm to earthworms and other beneficial insects. If you have ever had problems with seeds rotting in the ground or roots failing to take hold, treat your garden with one of these products, such as Mycostop or Root Shield, before planting.

CHAPTER 5
Healthy Harvest: Weeding, Pruning, Using

While many preparation and maintenance issues have already been mentioned throughout the book, here the focus is on what to do once your seedlings have sprouted and your garden has sprung. Following that are suggestions for what to do with the produce that you have on hand, with some quick and easy recipe ideas for making the most of your healthy harvest.

General Tips for Weeding

As with many great endeavors in life, preparation and prevention are almost as important as execution. That is, the best tip for keeping weeds in your garden under control: prevent them from growing rampant in the first place. The best way to do this is to, first, use a raised bed of some kind; this discourages weed growth by placing a healthy layer of topsoil over your subsoil. Second, block the weeds that will inevitably sprout from the subsoil by placing a barrier between your garden's subsoil and topsoil (good soil, compost, manure if using). The barriers can be made of anything that isn't chemically treated (which would be harmful to soil, groundwater, and plants, as well as subtracting from your proudly organic brand): old cardboard, a thick layer of newspapers, and biodegradable fabric will all work to varying degrees.

In addition, using a drip irrigation system is helpful: since the irrigation system is more pointedly directed at the plants you want to grow, it does not encourage grass seeds to grow willy-nilly. Smart planting will also help to impede weed growth: while you should avoid crowding your plants, of course, the close planting of desired crops leaves little room for the undesirable weeds.

Be aware, however, that no amount of preparation can prevent ALL weed growth. If you have a garden, weeds will inevitably grow. Your focus should be one keeping weed growth to a minimum, thus providing more room and more nutrients for your desired plants to grow.

So, when the inevitable weeds crop up, there are other ways to bring and keep them under control. Mulching your garden is always an effective barrier for weeds; plus, it provides temperature control for your topsoil, keeping it warm in cooler weather and shielding it from the direct heat of summer. Keep your mulch to a depth of about two inches, and beware: some commercial mulches may contain chemicals and/or be contaminated with weed seeds. Choose wisely.

Pulling weeds by hand will become a necessary effort at some point during the growing season. Some easy advice on how to manually weed effectively: weed in the dewy mornings or after a light rain, as wet soil releases the weed root more easily. Be sure to pull the weed up, root and all, or it will quickly grow back. Use a small garden trowel if your weeds get tough or aggressive, to help pull up grassroots without damaging nearby plant roots. Weed often! The longer the weed has to settle into your soil, the harder it will be to yank up.

Last, while it isn't clearly understood as to why this may be, most horticulturists will acknowledge that organic gardens with lots of good compost simply don't sprout as many weeds. Healthy soil makes for a healthy garden.

General Tips for Pruning

While pruning is not really the most important concern for a vegetable garden—it is more about the harvesting—there are some simple tips that you can use for your entire backyard to keep it looking good and growing well.

If you have perennials planted in your garden—things like mint or chives—then be sure to prune them back at the end of the growing season, so the dead material does not over mulch the soil and prevent new growth from cropping up next season. Also prune any dead growth that you may see during the season (although be aware that if you appear to have "dead" growth on one of your plants during the season, it is often indicative of disease). Last, do be sure to top any flowering plants, such as basil and lettuces, during the growing season, to keep them producing and avoid going to seed.

What not to do in terms of pruning in a vegetable garden may be even more important: no matter how tempting it may be to prune back vine-growing plants (tomatoes, cucumbers, squash, beans, peas), *do not do it*. While very occasionally helpful, most often this kind of pruning stunts growth of fruits or vegetables and can introduce disease.

How to Use Your Harvest

Finally! After all the work, the hours, the days, the months, you are able to enjoy the fruits of your labors, quite literally. This is the most satisfying and rewarding—nay, delicious—part of gardening. Below you will find some basic tips of harvesting your plants and how to use them once you have them happily lined up on your kitchen countertops. The following suggestions are not "recipes," per se, with an exact list of ingredients and measurements, but merely methods of preparing certain dishes focusing on what you've harvested. These methods are ripe for improvisation and substitution, so channel your creative energies!

Herbs:

When harvesting herbs, the general rule of thumb is to harvest only as much as you need at the time (that's the point of having them in the backyard, no?). If you do happen to gather a little too enthusiastically, avoid the refrigerator; instead, put the extra cut herbs in a glass of water and place in a windowsill (or, alternately, use an herb arrangement as a centerpiece for your dinner table: lovely and practical). Be sure, when gathering herbs, that you snip or cut them; don't pinch or pull them, which can introduce disease.

Dishes with Herbal Starring Roles

The first preparation that inevitably springs to mind when thinking of fresh garden herbs is **pesto**. While not really a stand-alone dish, it can be a star of dinner in its own right, adding layers of bright flavor not only when tossed with pasta but also when spooned over grilled steak or chop, swirled into soup, or stirred into a grain salad. A basic ratio of about 2 cups of herbs, with a ½ cup of nuts, a couple of garlic cloves, some acidity (lemon, lime, orange, light vinegar) to taste, and about a ¾ cup of quality olive oil. Cheese can be added, depending on what you're serving it with, usually about ½ cup hard cheeses, such as parmesan or pecorino. Whirl this together in a food processor or blender, or if you're lucky enough to have a good mortar and pestle, take the time to grind together slowly by hand. This latter, old-fashioned method produces a superlatively creamy pesto.

While most people automatically think first of the classic basil and pine nuts pairing when considering pesto, many other herb-nut combinations are wonderful in this kind of preparation, as well: think mint and walnuts, especially well-suited for spooning over lamb chops; parsley and pecans, great with steak; or chives/garlic chives and peanuts, to add an Asian flair. Also consider arugula, that spicy green, for pesto; it makes for a robust accompaniment to grilled meats or fish.

You can also make a great **salad** using your herbal bounty. A mix of tender young herb leaves tossed with a light vinaigrette and topped with some delicate shavings of cheese, or grated nuts is a lovely starter for any occasion. I love a mix of parsley and mint (3 to 1) with a lemon-based vinaigrette of 1 part lemon to 2 parts oil, with a splash of Dijon mustard and honey for emulsification and balance. A little smoked Spanish paprika (pimentón) adds a touch of sweet heat if you have it on hand, and salt to taste. Shave some hard cheese over with a vegetable peeler, letting it curl nicely, and/or grate some toasted pecans or walnuts over with a rasp. Beautiful, healthy, and delicious!

Another famously herb-forward dish in the salad category is **tabouli**. While many Americanized versions contain a lot of other ingredients—and there is nothing wrong with this, but still—the traditional version contains copious amounts of herbs with just a bit of bulgur wheat, lots of lemon and oil, some onion and maybe some tomato. Really, for a truly traditional Middle Eastern tabouli, you need only about ¼ cup of bulgur wheat, soaked or steamed until tender (a tip, if you have the time: soak the bulgur in lemon and olive oil along with a chopped tomato, if using, for several hours rather than steaming or boiling; it softens the bulgur while allowing it to absorb more flavor). To that amount of bulgur, add 2 cups herbs—chopped by hand! no processing!—and douse with equal parts of lemon juice and quality olive oil (1/3-1/2 cup of each). I like to use 1 cup parsley, ½ cup mint, and ½ cup cilantro. Add a small onion, chopped, or sliced scallions (about a ½ cup) and a tomato, chopped if you like. There is no better tabouli on earth than one made with herbs fresh from the garden.

Herbal **teas or tisanes** are yet another excellent way to make use of your herbs. I can tell you from firsthand experience, that fresh mint tea with lots of sugar is as good an afternoon pick-me-up as any other. Simply pour lightly boiling water over a handful of fresh leaves, add sugar to taste, and if you're squeamish, sieve out the leaves after steeping for a few minutes. You can also add some green tea leaves or bags to this to amp up flavor and caffeine content. Another wonderful herb for tea is lemon verbena, a rarer herb that is quite strong when raw but fragrant and tasty when used for tea.

Lastly, you can use your herbal bounty to make **flavored syrups**—a fine way to save your herbs for use after the season is over. Make a sugar syrup by lightly boiling equal amounts of sugar and water (add a touch more water if using a coarser raw sugar), then add a handful of fresh herbs to that and steep until cool room temperature. Strained and refrigerated in a sterilized jar, this will keep for several months. Again, lemon verbena is lovely in this preparation, as is lavender, mint, and basil. You can riff on this method by steeping citrus peels along with your herbs (lime loves mint, while basil enjoys lemon). If you're feeling fancy, add half a vanilla bean to any of these for the extraordinary depth of flavor. Use these syrups to flavor tea and cocktails, drizzle over dessert, or make sorbet.

Of course, herbs are the crowning touch of many a dish, adding a distinct freshness of flavor to nearly anything, and you'll find countless uses for the ones you have in your backyard. Roast chicken stuffed with tarragon; rolled omelet with chives; bread stuffing laced with lots of oregano and sage are just a few ideas for more ways to highlight your herbs.

Vegetables:

Lettuces

Obviously, the first thing that comes to mind when thinking about lettuce is a salad. A simple green salad with freshly picked lettuce is a true glory of spring and early fall. One caveat for using homegrown lettuces: *wash well!* Your lettuce will have dirt in it, undoubtedly (sometimes a critter or two), and while in an organic garden that dirt isn't perhaps too hazardous to your health, it is certainly unpleasantly gritty and not very tasty. The best way to wash lettuces (and greens) is to fill a clean sink full of cold water and add your lettuce; swish around for a minute, then let everything settle (the loose dirt will sink to the bottom of the sink). Carefully scoop out the lettuce with your hands, taking care not to disturb the dirt at the bottom, and let drain on clean dish towels. If you harvest after a rain, I'd recommend doing that two or three times. Then, rinse lettuce again, just to be sure you've dislodged all grit and spin in a salad spinner. You can store lettuce in the fridge for an afternoon or overnight—the cold can make lettuce exceptionally crisp—rolled up in a clean flour sack towel; spread the lettuce over the entire towel, leaving some border, then carefully roll up. The towel absorbs excess moisture while providing a protective layer against other fridge odors.

To dress your lettuce, you need nothing more than a bit of acid, some oil and a pinch of salt. Two tips on **vinaigrettes** that I've picked up via my travels: first, make a vinaigrette directly in your—very large!—salad bowl. Rub the bowl with a cut clove of garlic, add some Dijon mustard, and one part acid (lemon, white or red wine vinegar, sherry or balsamic vinegar) to two parts oil (extra virgin olive oil or walnut oil). Second, a lot of older recipes call for one part acid to three parts oil; for contemporary cooks, and especially on light and fresh lettuce, that feels heavy. Keep it 1:2 for best results.

Another important **dressing** to have in your repertoire is homemade ranch: trust me, you will never buy the bottled stuff again (and, if you ask me, it is nearly criminal to use chemically laden bottled dressing on fresh, organic lettuce). Basically, mix equal parts mayonnaise and buttermilk (let us say a ½ cup of each) to a clean jar, add a couple of tablespoons each of freshly minced parsley and chives, and about half a teaspoon each of garlic salt and onion salt. Shake well to mix. Add more mayo if too thin, more buttermilk if too thick, and more seasoning if you desire. Add some blue cheese to this for your cobb salad or buffalo wing dip; or, puree with some tarragon and avocado for green goddess-style dressing. This will keep in the fridge for a couple of weeks, though I doubt it will last that long.

Greens

Perhaps my favorite early spring and late fall harvest, greens can be light and crunchy, rich and velvety, star and side, depending on how you wish to prepare them. Again, as with lettuce, the first step in creating good food from garden greens is to *wash well!* See the above section on lettuces for some simple instructions on how to ensure that your greens are clean. I'd say that erring on the side of excess washing with greens, especially when consuming raw, is better than erring on the side of the deficit. Little worms love to live in the greens; if you see their tell-tale holes in any leaves, check your leaves well.

One of the first treats I make during the spring season is a **classic spinach salad** with warm bacon dressing. This method works well with arugula, too, or with a mix of spinach and arugula. Have ready a big bowl of cleaned spinach and to this add 4 or 5 thinly sliced mushrooms. Sauté 4 or 5 slices of bacon, chopped, in a skillet. When bacon is crisp and fat is rendered, whisk in 2 tablespoons of cider vinegar and a couple of teaspoons of brown sugar. Correct seasoning, if necessary (more vinegar and/or sugar, salt). Pour warm dressing over salad and toss well. Top with 2 or 3 sliced hard-boiled eggs. This is a full meal for two or a filling starter for four.

For a fall harvest of greens, one of my favorite things to do (besides traditional stewed collard greens: a Thanksgiving must) is to make a big pot of **Mediterranean style chard or kale**. Fill a large skillet—one that has a matching lid—to overflowing with cleaned chard and/or kale (you can mix them, but I find that using one or the other makes for a purer flavor). Don't bother to spin dry, as the water clinging to the leaves helps in cooking. To that add 1/3 cup of cilantro, one small bunch chopped scallions, a couple of minced garlic cloves, ¼ cup or more of quality olive oil, and a big tablespoon of smoked paprika. Let that wilt down over medium heat, stirring very carefully (as your pot should be literally overflowing with stuff), until the lid fits on top. Cover and turn to low heat; let cook for about 20-30 minutes for chard, 30-40 minutes for kale. You can turn this into a vegetarian main dish by throwing in a can of drained chickpeas.

There is also, of course, the Southern classic of **braised collard greens**. Though the methods for doing so are numerous, I happened upon a variation that I find even tastier than the traditional. Prepare your greens for stewing by stacking leaves then rolling them into a cigar shape and slicing; this a quick way to prep when you're using a bunch of greens. In a large pot, heat some olive oil and sauté the chopped onion and some chopped garlic (measurements depend on how many greens you're using and your own personal taste). Soften that a bit, then add collard greens by the handful and stir as each batch wilts slightly until all greens are incorporated and barely wilted. Throw in a smoked turkey wing—or, if you have access to some smoked duck, this is even better—and a cup or so of water. Cover and simmer for a couple of hours, then remove the wing and shred meat before returning to the pot. Add a few splashes of vinegar and some red pepper if you like a bit of spice. I used to do this when I had ducks from hunting trips. After smoking the duck, I'd reserve the wings and skin to add to collard greens. Rich and tasty while still being a bit lighter than the usual salt pork seasoning.

All greens lend themselves well to salads, though heartier greens such as mature Swiss chard, kale and collards must be treated a little differently. Thinly slice or finely chop these heartier greens and rub with a little coarse salt and lemon juice; let sit for an hour or so. The greens will soften a bit but remain crunchy. Toss with more juice, some oil, and salt to taste, and serve as is. Or add dried fruits, such as cranberries, and toasted nuts.

Sugar Snap Peas

As the name suggests, these little pods are sweet and neat, ready to eat out of hand. I always have a few right off the vine as a reward for my weeding efforts. You may want to "string" certain varieties by pinching the top off and pulling the fibrous string down the back of the pod, but it is only necessary if you find the fibrous string unpleasant.

I use sugar snap peas indiscriminately when they are in season, throwing them into salads or adding them to a quick sauté any time a few are at hand. They pair particularly well with radishes, and all you need to dress a salad of thinly sliced peas and radishes is some lemon and oil.

My favorite early spring dish with snaps is a **sautéed pea medley**: if you've grown garlic, pull up an early head or two; this immature garlic—green garlic it is called at the market—makes a wonderfully fragrant accompaniment. Cook your sliced green garlic or some spring onions in some good olive oil until softened, then toss in about a cup each of thinly sliced sugar snap peas and regular green peas (shelled or frozen). Cook until peas are tender yet still crisp. If your market has pea tendrils, fava beans, and/or green almonds, add them to the mix; the more, the merrier. Top with minced herbs of just about any kind: mint, parsley, and/or tarragon are fantastic.

I also love them with steak salad, such as **Thai beef salad**: if you have leftover grilled steak, slice thinly and toss with crisp lettuce and sliced sugar snap peas. Make a dressing with equal parts lime and soy sauce (or, better yet, half soy sauce, half fish sauce), and throw in some minced garlic and hot green chiles—the spicier, the better in my household. Whisk in a dash of sugar and pour over vegetables and steak. The green vegetal taste of the snaps really sings in this salty, funky, spicy dressing.

But they are also excellent when **sautéed or roasted** quickly in a hot oven. Simply coat with oil and sauté over high heat or blast-roast in a really hot oven. When lightly blistered, toss with a dash of toasted sesame oil and salt, then sprinkle with sesame seeds.

Radishes

Crunchy and lightly spicy, the radish is yet another lovely spring vegetable that livens up any number of salads. Like sugar snap peas, they can be eaten out of hand with little to no preparation (just, of course, some cleaning). As mentioned above they are great paired with sugar snap peas and these two can be substituted for each other in any number of recipes.

My go-to recipe for radishes is a **crunchy relish**, one that pairs so well with spring lamb or pork that I find myself making it several times throughout spring and fall. A food processor is best for this, but chopping by hand can certainly work if a little more time-consuming. Throw about 10 trimmed radishes in your processor, along with about ¼ cup mint and/or parsley and/or a mix. Add ¼ cup nuts and a couple of tablespoons of lemon juice and olive oil and pulse until coarsely chopped (adjust texture according to how you're serving it: coarse for a salad-like presentation, finer for a relish). I use local pecans for this, and sometimes add a seeded jalapeno and a minced clove or two of garlic for a stronger flavor. Not only lovely spooned alongside grilled lamb or pork chop but also tasty spooned into cooled, cooked rice with a dash of mayonnaise to combine (add some drained tuna for a non-vegetarian lunch).

Another extraordinary thing to do with radishes, particularly the **French breakfast radish**, is to simply wash and trim radishes that have been refrigerated until cold. Serve whole or halved alongside a pot of the best butter you can buy or make and a saucer of coarse sea salt. Dip radishes in butter then dab into salt. With some fresh baguette and charcuterie, a heavenly lunch.

For an **Asian riff on the radish side dish**, trim and halve radishes (quarter if large), then soak in equal parts red wine vinegar and soy sauce for about an hour, turning a couple of times. Salty, sour, crunchy counterpart to a stir-fry or a curry.

Cruciferous Vegetables

One of the last vegetables to mature in the spring or fall seasons, cabbages, broccoli and cauliflower, and Brussel sprouts are both sweeter and heartier when homegrown. Almost every cook has a recipe or two in their pocket for these common vegetables; hopefully, these few methods will give you some new ideas for how to use them.

Fresh, sweet cabbage from the garden just begs for some **coleslaw**, and most ambitious home cooks have a recipe they use already. I like to thinly slice the cabbage and salt it first, leaving it to stand and drain in a colander for an hour or two; this ensures that the final slaw isn't watered down. Some people add carrots or purple cabbage to their slaw, and this is fine—and pretty—but when I have fresh garden cabbage, I like to leave it the lone star. I just add a minimal amount of mayonnaise, some cider vinegar, and a bit of sugar; I like the slaw to taste of cabbage, not mayo and tart-sweet as opposed to sweet-tart. Toss in some chopped toasted pecans to deepen the flavor, and/or some fresh herbs to freshen.

Raw cabbage is also **exceptional on tacos**—better than delicate lettuce which gets overwhelmed by the spicier, meatier flavor of most tacos. Toss with lime and salt before topping your taco or tostada.

Cabbage can also be cooked—though many don't enjoy the sulfurous odor of cooked cabbage—and I adore **Southern-style smothered cabbage**. Simply chop an onion and a small head of cabbage and add to a big skillet, along with more butter than you think you should use (a good half stick). Sprinkle with salt and coarse pepper, cover, and cook it over low for 45 minutes or more. Take the lid off, raise heat and let it brown up a bit.

Broccoli, cauliflower, and Brussel sprouts all take exceptionally well to roasting; this creates a caramelized and even crunchy exterior while keeping the vegetable juicy and rendering it tender. As each takes different lengths of time to roast, I don't recommend cooking them as a medley; also, don't crowd the pan when roasting for best results. Use a sheet pan, if you have it, lined with aluminum foil. Toss broccoli or cauliflower heads or halve Brussel sprouts in enough quality olive oil to coat and roast at 425 degrees for 30-45 minutes, until browned. Any of these are great as a side dish, as is, but they also take well to some post-roasting additions: broccoli with pine nuts and pecorino cheese; cauliflower with capers and walnuts; Brussel sprouts with a splash of fish sauce and some Asian chile powder (shichimi togarashi, for example) sprinkled with toasted rice Krispies. I know the latter sounds odd, but it is truly delicious, inspired by David Chang of Momofuku.

I also like to make **a broccoli-cauliflower casserole**. Blanch equal parts broccoli and cauliflower in boiling salted water for a couple of minutes (don't overcook or your casserole will be mushy); drain well. Make a basic béchamel sauce with butter, flour, and milk. For about a cup of béchamel, mix equal parts butter and flour (2 tablespoons) and cook over medium heat until flour starts to color a bit, then whisk in a cup of milk slowly, stirring constantly to prevent lumps. Toss your vegetables with the béchamel, put in a greased baking pan—thinly spread out if you like the crunchy bits—and top with grated Gruyere cheese and a sprinkle of panko bread crumbs. You can use other cheeses, but the Gruyere really complements the flavor of the broccoli-cauliflower mixture.

Another great way to use broccoli and/or cauliflower is in **soup**: this is an especially handy way to make sure that excess produce does not go to waste, as soup freezes well. All you need is a head of broccoli or cauliflower, a small onion, and some good quality vegetable or chicken stock. You can leave chunky or puree (use an immersion blender for a quick coarse puree or whirl in a processor or blender). Whatever else you add is up to you: potatoes or rice for some starchy bulk; milk or cream for a silky-smooth puree; some diced tomatoes and/or a handful of fresh corn kernels for acidity and sweetness; or, as my mom couldn't resist, a hefty serving of cheese. She used Velveeta for which I will forgive her (I still love her version, despite my better instincts), but a good melting cheddar elevates the idea a bit.

Pole (Green) Beans

Sitting on a cool back porch snapping beans is certainly a revered summer pastime. It is a chance to reflect on the spring that has just passed while not worrying too terribly much about the summer heat and potential drought to come.

There are two basic ways I like to cook green beans: blanched and stewed. Blanching lends itself to endless variety, as you can toss quickly **blanched beans** with any number of vinaigrettes and add-ins. Simply blanch beans in boiling salted water to the desired doneness, 2 minutes for crisp and up to 5 minutes for near-tender. Plunge immediately into a bowl of ice water to stop cooking and preserve the color. These can be kept in the fridge for a day or two before using; or frozen for later in the year (more on that in the next chapter). Dress with a red wine vinaigrette and toss in a bunch of slivered basil and some minced garlic for an excellent side salad. Or, toss with a walnut-oil vinaigrette and a handful of chopped toasted walnuts.

Green bean and potato stew is one of the glories of Southern cooking, and it wouldn't be summer without making a couple of pots of this. Coarsely chop a 12-ounce package of bacon and add a pound of snapped green beans and a pound of new potatoes, halved if on the larger side. Throw in a cup of water, some salt and pepper, and simmer lightly for an hour or so. Dead simple cooking that requires only the increasingly rarest of treats: absolutely fresh vegetables.

Okra

Onto the height of summer, the almost invincible okra will pop up and proliferate in what seems like minutes. Of course, almost everyone knows that fried okra is the way to go, but there are a couple of possible variations on that theme, as well as some lovely stewed preparations that are wonderful with okra.

One of the not-so-secret characteristics of okra—its sliminess—can be either a boon or a bane, depending on what you're cooking. That gelatinous character can be an excellent thickener (think gumbo), but in quick, stand-alone preparations it can be off-putting. A secret: leave the top of the pod alone. **Traditional fried okra** calls for cutting okra into rounds and tossing with cornmeal, or a mix of cornmeal and flour, and pan-frying in vegetable oil. This is excellent, of course, but for virtually slime-free results, cut pods in half, leaving top trimmed but intact. For **Asian fried okra**, don't dredge in flour but pan fry, halved, over high heat. You want the okra to be nearly burned. Toss with minced garlic and hot chiles, some chopped fresh basil and/or cilantro and season with some fish sauce or salt. Prepared this way, okra can be served as an hors d'oeuvres.

Certainly, if you ever make gumbo, okra is a must-have ingredient (well, some people use file powder, but they certainly wouldn't if they had Cajun relatives). But **stewed okra and tomatoes** is another fine way to use some of your bountiful crop. Put whole okra pods in a pot—smaller is better for this dish—and add about half as many (by volume) chopped tomatoes; pour in a glug of olive oil and let simmer for about 30-40 minutes, until tomatoes have dissolved and created a kind of sauce for okra. The long cooking time, plus the whole pod preparation, eliminates the typical mucilaginous texture. Add some fresh herbs and a squeeze of lemon for brightness.

Tomatoes

The uses for garden ripe tomatoes are endless, and even when unripe (fried green tomatoes, anyone?), tomatoes have their uses. It would be easily possible to pen an entire book just on the use of tomatoes, but I'll limit myself to a few quick and simple preparations, alongside a couple of more involved but less typical ideas. See the following chapter for methods using tomatoes for preservation, such as sauce preparations.

By far the easiest and most anticipated way to eat tomatoes—after a long winter and spring, deprived of the joys of a perfectly ripe, just off-the-vine tomato—is to **slice and serve**. Friends of mine beg for sliced tomatoes arranged on a platter, drizzled with the best olive oil I can afford, a splash of sherry vinegar (most people use balsamic; that's fine, too), some slivered basil, and a sprinkle of blue cheese. The variations are virtually endless: intersperse sliced mozzarella (or, better yet, burrata) with tomato slices and shower with basil; scatter some capers (fried until crisp, if you're up to it) and olives over your platter of tomatoes; make a cheese cracker dough (equal parts flour, butter, and cheese), bake in a pie pan, and layer drained slice tomatoes on top. Just about any salty, savory, umami-laden ingredients, you can fish out of your pantry or fridge goes well with tomatoes.

Of course, you will usually have **cherry tomatoes** first, and these are great added to any salad or marinated in oil and vinegar (with garlic and herbs or not) and served as a side on their own. But if you end up with too many to eat out of hand, roasted cherry tomatoes are absolutely delicious with grilled meats, especially fish: in a baking dish large enough to hold a single layer, throw in your cherry tomatoes and enough good olive oil to coat; there's no need to halve them, but I do recommend you use a paring knife or skewer to poke a tiny hole in each, to prevent bursting and splattering. Splash with some sherry vinegar, tuck in some whole peeled garlic cloves, and top with several sprigs of oregano. Roast at 350 degrees for 30-40 minutes, until tomatoes have broken down and garlic is soft. Mash together or leave chunky, depending on how you serve it. Great smeared on toasted bread, as well.

Of course, you can't have fresh summer tomatoes without making a **salsa** or two: Mexican style with jalapenos, garlic, cilantro and lime; Italian style with olive oil, balsamic vinegar, garlic and basil; Middle Eastern style with olive oil, lots of lemon juice and tons of fresh parsley.

A world-famous preparation of tomatoes has to be **gazpacho**, and there are many variations on that theme, from the thin Andalusian-style cold soup to the thicker salmorejo style originating from

Cordoba. There are also endless variations that have roots in the American Southwest. I am a purist when it comes to gazpacho, given that I have an ample supply of vine-ripened heirloom tomatoes. In its simplest form, tomatoes, excellent olive oil, and aged sherry vinegar are pureed and strained; poured around a cold seafood salad and some sliced avocado, this is truly shatteringly good, but dependent wholly on ingredients. Most Andalusian-style gazpacho recipes call for some water-soaked bread to act as a thickener, and perhaps some cucumber and bell pepper to boot. Salmorejo is simply a thicker version, with more bread to tomato ratio, and usually topped with crunchy croutons, chopped hard boiled egg, and crisped Serrano ham.

A cousin to gazpacho is a **Moroccan-inspired cold tomato soup** that incorporates some spicier elements. Heat a tablespoon of olive oil and gently cook a few minced garlic cloves and a couple of teaspoons each of smoked paprika and ground cumin until garlic softens and the mixture is fragrant. Grate a couple of pounds of tomatoes (or pass through a food mill, if you have one), then add the oil-spice mixture, some chopped cilantro, and a couple of stalks of diced celery. Add some lemon juice for brightens, salt to taste, and stir in a bit of water to thin, if you deem it necessary. Serve very cold.

Grated tomatoes also make an excellent marinade, with the addition of some acid and oil, perhaps some garlic and herbs. The tomatoes help tenderize the meat when marinated. I especially like to do this with chicken, to be grilled kebab style.

During the height of the season, I'm mostly indulging in raw preparations of tomatoes, but there are a couple of exceptions. If I have the grill going, some **stuffed tomatoes** are always a delicious side: put halved and seeded tomatoes into a baking pan that you don't mind putting on the grill, drizzle with olive oil and stuff with a mixture of equal parts bread crumbs and grated parmesan, streaked through with chopped herbs (basil and oregano good, but tarragon also works for a different flavor). Place on grill until tomatoes wilt and cheese begins to brown. This can also be done in an oven, of course.

Cucumbers

Cucumbers, like tomatoes, are one of the summer's delights and can be prepared with simplicity and ease for an excellent fresh crunch to any meal. Slice and serve is great, with only a splash of vinegar and some salt needed to make a side dish for just about any meal.

Quick pickles are also useful to have on hand, to have on the side, in a sandwich, or as a relish. I like to seed my cucumbers for most recipes, as the seeds can be hard to digest. Peel and seed a couple of cucumbers (leave the peel on if the early season and cucumbers are young and tender); toss in a bowl with enough vinegar to coat, and season with equal parts salt and sugar. Place into a baggie and tightly seal, squeezing all the air out. These can be eaten within a few hours and up to a couple of days after preparing, and obviously take well to other seasonings, if you like.

Cucumber salsa is also a refreshing break from the usual tomato-based salsas. Excellent with spicy grilled meats, one of my favorites goes well with jerk chicken or pork. Stir together 1 part cucumber to half mango; add enough oil to coat. Season with salt and toss in fresh herbs (thyme is really nice here), some minced scallion or onion, and some seeded chile peppers.

Melons

Melons, like the other summer fruits detailed above, are also quick and easy to eat: peel and cut or halve, seed, and eat with a spoon. Some classic preparations include cantaloupe-style melon cut into wedges and draped with prosciutto or serrano ham; pickled melon rind; and a reminder of old Americana, melon with cottage cheese. Melon can also be treated just like tomatoes and cucumbers and make good savory salads and salsas.

One other preparation popular in Latin American cultures is the **melon cooler**—one of many *agua frescas*—served in markets and restaurants. Fill a blender nearly full with cubed melon, add ¼ to a ½ cup of sugar (depending on how sweet your melon is), and a couple of tablespoons of lime juice. Puree until very smooth, then pour into a couple of pitchers and add a cup of ice water to each pitcher. Adjust with more sugar and/or lime to taste.

Chile & Other Peppers

Chiles and other peppers are usually relegated to supporting ingredients, and many renowned cuisines would not be the same without these hearty new world ingredients. Fresh chiles are crucial to salsas and add a punch to stir fry and curries.

Many dishes call for peppers to be **roasted**, then peeled and seeded before use: the roasting intensifies the flavor of the chile, and adds a subtle smokiness as well. There are a couple of ways to do this. If you are only roasting a couple of chiles for a dish and have a gas stove, simply take the ring off the stove and, using heat proof tongs, roast the chiles directly in the flame for a few seconds on each side until the skin blackens and the chiles smell fragrant. Alternatively, place an oven rack at the topmost part of your oven and heat oven to 450 degrees. Roast chiles directly on oven rack, turning once or twice until skins are charred. If you are roasting a lot of chiles—for a batch of stew or sauce or for freezing—use a large sheet pan lined with foil. In this case, you might want to halve and seed your chiles before roasting, placing them on a sheet in a single layer. This eliminates the need to turn chiles, as well as making de-seeding simpler. For ease of peeling, place roasted peppers in a paper bag to let steam for a few minutes after roasting.

Peppers can also be **stuffed**, as in the ubiquitous jalapeno poppers on menus of the recent past, or in more refined dishes such as chiles en nogada, the Mexican specialty served at the holidays. I like to make **chile rellenos** when I have decent-sized Anaheims or poblanos in the garden: after roasting and peeling, stuff peppers with cheese or ground beef cooked with garlic and cumin (or a mix), then carefully coat in a tempura batter and deep fry until batter puffs and cheese melts. I keep a quick tempura batter mix on hand: mix together three cups cake flour with a ¾ cup of cornstarch and leaven with a couple of teaspoons of baking soda; add a teaspoon or two of salt. When ready to use, mix with seltzer water to form a batter (usually, a ration of two parts batter to one part liquid). Serve chiles rellenos with a smooth enchilada style sauce or fresh salsa, if you have it.

Squash & the Like

Squash is another prolific crop, whether in summer (yellow crookneck, zucchini) or fall (acorn, butternut). Squash is virtually foolproof to grow and lends itself to any number of simple recipes.

Zucchini-corn sauté is one of my favorites; it makes an excellent vegetable side dish to put out on a table laden with enchiladas or tacos. Slice a couple of zucchinis into half-moons, then sauté in a large skillet for a couple of minutes; throw in a cup or so of corn kernels, preferably fresh off the cob, and increase heat, cooking until both zucchini and corn start to brown. Finish with a squeeze of lime juice and a shower of chopped cilantro.

Squash can also be hollowed out and **stuffed**, then baked, for an elegant side dish to a summer meal. Sauté the squash insides with garlic, onion, and herbs, then stir in cooked rice or crispy breadcrumbs and return to squash shells. Sprinkle with more breadcrumbs and/or grated hard cheese, and bake until shells are tender. Sometimes I add some black olives to the mix for some salty punch.

Acorn squash is a beautiful fall squash that works well for stuffing: simply cut in half and scoop out stringy flesh and seeds, then add a filling: a big pat of butter and some cinnamon mixed with brown sugar, or some crumbled Italian sausage spiked with maple syrup. Note that the squash is left unpeeled, but the skins aren't meant for eating; scoop out servings, or serve half a squash as a full entrée. Be sure to slice a piece off the underside of the squash, so it sits flat while baking.

Alliums (Garlic & Onions & Leeks)

Another group of supporting players, alliums show up just about everywhere in cooking. Here are a couple of recipe ideas that highlight each of these usually supporting players.

Chicken with 40 cloves of garlic is a famous French preparation and a delicious way to make your house smell warm and inviting. Basically, this is just a garlicky roast chicken. I like to spatchcock a whole chicken (this is the process by which you remove the backbone, then flip the chicken and break the breastbone, thus flattening it—makes for more even cooking) but you can cut a whole chicken into pieces if you'd rather. Pour a thin layer of olive oil into a roasting pan and add your chicken or chicken pieces, skin side up. Scatter peeled garlic cloves around and some sprigs of fresh chicken or tarragon, if you like. Cover with foil (or use an oven-safe pan with a lid) and cook at 350 degrees until done, about an hour. Make sure you have plenty of good crusty bread to spread the soft garlic cloves on.

Caramelized onions are one of those kitchen staples that are always wonderful to have around: make more than you think you'll need and freeze for later use. All you need is a nonstick pan, preferably, some butter and/or oil, lots of onions of any color, and some patience. Cook sliced onions in butter or oil (I use a mix) over relatively low heat, stirring occasionally until they get really dark brown, up to an hour and a half. Serve with grilled meats, atop burgers and sausages, or add to homemade pizza.

When leeks and potatoes come together during the season, I always think of **vichyssoise**, the cold pureed French soup. It is easy to make and light yet filling. Sauté equal parts leeks and potatoes in some butter (only use white and light green parts of leek and peel potatoes). Add chicken stock to cover and toss in a bay leaf and some herb sprigs, if you like. Simmer until leeks and potatoes are very tender. Puree in blender until smooth, then allow to cool and add a bit of cream or half and half. Chill, and serve with sliced chives on top. For about 4 servings use 5 leeks, 5 potatoes, and 5 cups of chicken stock.

Potatoes

This hearty vegetable, ubiquitous on the American table, lends itself to almost any preparation: baked, boiled, fried, roasted, scalloped, and pancaked, most home cooks have a handy set of potato recipes on call. I've already mentioned them as co-stars in such dishes as green bean and potato stew and potato-leek soup (vichyssoise). Some more out of the ordinary recipes for the humble spud follow.

While it is not often that we think of the potato as a suitable vegetable for stir-frying, there are many places in China that have adopted the potato; in the southern part of China, you'll find **Sichuan-style stir-fried potatoes**. Cooked quickly and left slightly crunchy, these potatoes are very different than your average roasted or baked potatoes. Peel and cut about a pound and a half of potatoes into slivers, like matchsticks. Soak them for a while in cold salted water to remove starch. Drain well. Heat oil in a wok or heavy skillet until very hot, then cook a half a dozen small dried red chiles (leave them whole) and a teaspoon or two Sichuan peppercorns for a couple of minutes until fragrant. Add matchstick potatoes and some salt and stir fry for about another 5 minutes. Drizzle with some toasted sesame oil and serve.

Another fun and different way to prepare potatoes hails from Spain. Best with small red or white potatoes—creamy not fluffy potatoes—**patatas bravas** (brave potatoes) are a ubiquitous part of a tapas-style spread. Boil potatoes whole until tender, then lightly smash and coat with oil. Spread in a single layer on a baking sheet and roast in a 450-degree oven for 35-45 minutes, until potatoes are very brown and crunchy. Meanwhile, make the brava sauce: sauté a small chopped onion, some chopped garlic, and a can of tomatoes (or use your own, roasted and peeled) until onion is very tender. Cool slightly then puree in blender or processor with a couple of teaspoons smoked paprika. Serve over potatoes, or on the side for dipping, along with homemade mayonnaise. (You don't know how to make homemade mayonnaise? It's easy and delicious: whirl one egg, one egg yolk, some lemon juice and a splash of Dijon mustard and some salt in blender or processor until just mixed. Slowly—*slowly*—drizzle in *very fresh* olive oil, about a ¾ cup, until mixture is emulsified.)

CHAPTER 6
Preserving Your Produce: Strategies for Zero Waste Gardening

After months of hard work—planning, planting, growing—the last thing a gardener wants is to let any of his or her harvest to go to waste. If, like me, you have a relatively small plot on which you're planting just a few items, then you may easily be able to use everything you grow as you pick it. However, if, like me, you turn out to be better than expected at the gardening endeavor—an unexpected pleasure—then you may have to come up with ways in which your crops aren't wasted. In addition, many people, again like me, simply wish to preserve something of spring and summer to hold them over the long winter months. February is perhaps the dreariest month of the year (unless you live in southern Arizona), and nothing lifts the spirits as much as cracking open a can of cucumber pickles or rescuing a freezer bag full of homemade tomato sauce. There are many methods by which you can successfully maintain a "zero waste" garden, from the complex to the simple.

Lest we forget: one of the simplest ways to ensure that not a single fruit, vegetable, stem, or vine goes to waste in your garden is to feed your compost pile. Any inedible or undesirable bits of skin or core or bird-picked fruit should be tossed in the pile (or, alas, the occasional neglected scrap at the bottom of the vegetable bin). When one season rolls into another and you are clearing away the last roots from your spring plants or vines from your summer plants, be sure to grind these up as best you can and add them to the pile, as well. Each year your garden is fed by the garden of yesteryear, a true cycle of life (to paraphrase a famous film).

Other ingenious ways to keep your crops throughout the year are as follows: canning, freezing, dehydrating (drying), fermenting, and smoking. See details on each method, plus some recipe suggestions, below.

Canning

A nearly foolproof way to preserve your harvest for months—even years—to come, canning is a lost art among most home cooks. Supermarkets have made it far too easy to obtain whatever produce you want at whatever time of year you desire it. While there is nothing inherently wrong with this, it is certainly economically and environmentally sound to grow your own food and to preserve it. Canning is a time-honored way to do just that.

For canning, you do need a little specialized equipment, such as a water bath canner and/or a pressure canner, canning jars (mason jars, such as Ball and Kerr) with lids, and a jar lifter. If you become very serious about canning, be aware that there are two types of canning deemed safe for long term preservation: water bath canning for high acid products and pressure canning for low acid products. Thus, if you want to can your vegetables straight from your garden, you'll need to invest in a pressure canner. If you intend to can sauces or pickles or jellies made with the produce from your garden, a water bath canner should work. For details on how to obtain canning equipment and how to can safely, the Ball© Kerr© company provides an excellent site; click here for more information.

I have done some canning in my time, but I found I don't produce quite enough to justify the investment of time. Should you acquire a large parcel of land upon which to grow numerous plants of each variety, I urge you to learn. For those of us in suburban or urban areas with small raised beds, a more practical way of keeping fruits and vegetables through the winter is freezing.

Freezing

If, like me, you don't have the time, space, or equipment to do much canning, and you don't have a garden big enough to need to save a harvest for longer than a few months, freezing is the way to go. The only equipment you need besides your produce is sturdy storage bags—quart size is the best for ease of storage and size of portion—and a black sharpie.

While a lot of produce freezes well, some items are not as well suited. Freezing things like lettuce and radishes isn't recommended. A general rule to follow: if the produce can be blanched without altering its characteristics drastically, then it can be frozen. For example, green beans are excellent for freezing: simply blanch the green beans in boiling salted water for a couple of minutes; shock them quickly in ice water to halt cooking and preserve color; then dry and place on a sheet pan or cookie tray in a single layer; put into freezer until frozen; then pack into a freezer bag labeling the contents and—this is important—*the date on which it was frozen*. Most vegetables will keep well if stored properly for about six months, but after that, they start to lose flavor and can become frostbitten.

The **above blanching and freezing method** can also be used for sugar snap peas, broccoli, cauliflower, Brussel sprouts, and some low moisture squashes. Greens of various kinds take well to this, though the method is a little different: blanch hearty greens like kale and collards for about five minutes, while softer greens like spinach and chard only take a minute or two. When blanched, drain in a colander and rinse with cold water. Sometimes I throw a handful of ice cubes on top to speed the cooling process, but then you've got to pick bits of green off the cubes. I don't like using an ice bath on greens as I feel it tends to waterlog them a bit too much. When cool enough to handle, squeeze as much liquid as you can out of the greens, and coarsely chop before packing into a labeled freezer bag. Other vegetables, such as okra and cucumbers, are better served by pickling of some kind (see the fermenting section below for details on that).

Potatoes can also be frozen in this manner, for a french fry preparation. Blanch in hot oil until lightly cooked but not colored; drain well and pat dry before freezing in a single layer on a baking sheet. Put in your prepared freezer bags and, when ready to eat, cook them in hot oil (about 325 to 350 degrees) until browned and crunchy. No need to defrost.

Another method by which you can prepare certain crops for freezing is **roasting**. Roasted peppers are excellent candidates for freezing (see Chapter 5 for details on how to roast peppers), and I like to make a mixed bag of roasted peppers—jalapenos, poblanos, and anaheims—to pull out for making green chile stew during the winter. So, if you don't have enough of one kind for freezing, make a "house blend," as it were.

Tomatoes are also ideal for roasting, and I invariably put several freezer bags of both plain roasted tomatoes and tomato sauces away each season. For the best-roasted tomatoes, core each tomato and score an X in the bottom end; place tomatoes in a single layer on a foil-lined baking sheet, core side down. Roast near the top of the oven at 450 degrees for ten minutes or so (timing depends on the size and ripeness of tomatoes; use your best judgement, as there really isn't a way to fail at this), until the tomatoes emit juice and the X starts to curl the skin back. You want the skin to easily peel off but not for the tomatoes to fall to mush (though, if they do, no matter: still usable). When cool enough, peel and, if you like, squeeze the tomatoes to release most of the juice and seeds before packing into labeled freezer bags. This method most closely mimics what you would get in a supermarket can of whole tomatoes (though large heirloom varieties typically have a higher moisture content). Another tip: *don't throw away the juice from the roasted tomatoes!* Simply pass through a fine sieve to remove seeds and bits of the skin; add a bit of salt and lemon or lime juice to taste, and drink it for breakfast or in a glorious Bloody Mary.

I also like to make **sauces** from the roasted tomatoes. In a good harvest year, I put away three or four bags of plain roasted tomatoes and two or three bags each of three ready-made sauces I like to have on hand.

The first is a simple **Italian red sauce**, delicious on spaghetti with nothing more than a sprinkle of cheese or to add to baked pasta dishes or Italian-inspired roasts. Most years, just about every ingredient in this comes directly from my lovely little organic garden. Sauté a coarsely chopped yellow or white onion and garlic in some quality olive oil (be generous: it is Italian cooking, after all). When onion and garlic have softened a bit, add about 8 to 10 roasted, skinned, seeded tomatoes, crushing them lightly with your hands as you go. Throw in half a dozen large basil leaves, season with salt, and let lightly simmer for 20-30 minutes. You want flavors to meld and all the ingredients to be soft, but for some liquid to remain. Let everything cool, then whirl in the processor with another half dozen basil leaves. You could also use some oregano here, or a mix of basil and oregano. Since basil does not dry well, I use it in sauces and save oregano for drying. Put sauce in your labeled freezer bag: the above recipe should fit in your standard quart-sized bag.

The second is an even simpler **Mexican-inspired chipotle sauce** for enchiladas or fideo dishes. Simple puree 8 to 10 roasted, skinned, seeded tomatoes with 2 or 3 canned or homemade chipotle peppers (see below) and some salt. If you want a slightly more complex sauce, sauté some onion and garlic until soft and add to the above. Put into prepared freezer bags.

The third is a **Mediterranean-syle tomato sauce**, excellent with grilled meats and kebabs or as a sauce for meatballs or chickpeas. Sauté some chopped garlic in a generous amount of good olive oil in a small pan until softened, then add a couple of teaspoons each smoked paprika and cumin and a teaspoon of Aleppo pepper (a marvelous coarse flaked dried pepper with hints of tartness and mild heat: well worth seeking out). Let the mixture cook for a minute or two, until the spices "bloom," then pour over your roasted, skinned, seeded tomatoes (8 to 10) in a processor or blender. Give it some salt and pulse until combined. Add a squeeze of lemon if it needs some acid or a pinch of sugar if it needs some mellowing. Put into prepared freezer bags.

Again, all of these recipe suggestions can be canned in a pressure canner, should you have one.

Dehydrating (Drying)

Even if you don't own a specialized home dehydrator, there are a few simple ways to preserve certain items from your harvest for later. A dehydrator is a nice piece of equipment if you decide to embark on such things as fruit leathers or vegetable chips, but with just a little patience and care, you can stock your pantry through the winter.

The most obvious **candidates for dehydrating are herbs**, and drying your own herbs makes for a far superior product than the vast majority of commercially processed herbs on the market. Certain herbs take to drying more readily than others; basil and chives both lose too much flavor in the process (and basil tends to rot before it thoroughly dries), so I find those aren't worth the trouble. But tarragon, oregano, and mint take especially well to drying and the process couldn't be simpler: at the end of the growing season, pull up your plant if you don't wish to overwinter or cut it all back if you do (keep the mint, for sure) and wash well. It is nearly impossible to remove dust from dried leaves so don't skimp on the washing. Place the plants on a large sheet tray and stick it on top of your refrigerator (or another cool, dry place) for a couple of weeks. Once dry, strip the leaves off the plants in store in airtight containers away from sunlight. These should stay fresh and fragrant until next year's harvest.

Many people also utilize a microwave for quick drying. It is considerably faster—just microwave in short ten second bursts until herbs are dried—though I always fear I might "cook" the herbs instead of preserving their fresh flavor. **Oven drying** over the lowest heat is also another way in which to dry herbs and other small crops; this can take from two hours to ten hours depending on what you're drying. Again, this kind of heat-based drying will change the characteristics somewhat. That said, oven drying is excellent for making "sun-dried" tomatoes, with smaller paste tomatoes such as the Roma.

The **other prime candidates for drying are peppers**. Once you've made your own pure chile powders, you will inevitably be disappointed by most commercial brands. With cayenne peppers, I make a *ristra* (wreath) of peppers, threading them onto a string as they become ripe throughout the season. To thread peppers, simply push a needle threaded with a double layer of sturdy string that's been tied off at the end through the stem of the pepper, slide it down, then slide the next one. Hang this from your kitchen windowsill or other sunny spot where you will not forget it. As I said, just add as peppers turn a bright red and once growing season is over and all are nicely dried, grind in a clean coffee or spice grinder until the consistency is to your liking. Save some whole, if you like, to throw into soups, stews, stocks or stir-fries for a bit of a punch.

The above *ristra* method works well for small, skinny peppers but not as efficiently for thicker, juicier peppers such as jalapenos and poblanos. These peppers are more likely to rot before they dry—unless you have a dehydrator—because of their size and moisture content. In addition, these peppers are typically used in smoked form, transforming into chipotles and anchos, respectively. See below for quick ideas.

Smoking

If you have a backyard smoker, smoking is another effective way to preserve certain crops. It is essentially an intensive way of drying foods while adding the layer of smoke flavor. If you don't have a backyard smoker or wood-fired grill, a propane grill can be used, though it will burn through a good bit of fuel in the process.

Whenever you get prepared to do some smoking, remember your garden: prepare a *ristra* of jalapenos and/or poblanos. Typically, this is done when these peppers are very ripe and have turned red. When still green, they are used fresh or roasted. Make sure they are hanging quite close together so the string will not burn and cut a long slit in each pepper to encourage the juices to drip out more quickly. (In fact, it is best if you harvest the peppers a week or so in advance and let them dry out a bit before smoking; this speeds the time they'll spend in the pit.) When they have shriveled and hardened, take them off the smoker. Make sure they are devoid of moisture, or they can spoil (if they are still somewhat moist, throw them in prepared freezer bags; they'll still be great).

Dried chipotles can be used like commercial canned chipotles, though they will need to be rehydrated in soaking liquid first. They will not taste quite the same without the adobo sauce that coats them in the can, though you can make your own and store your dried chipotles in it for a couple of months in the fridge. It is usually a mix of tomatoes, onions, garlic, cumin, oregano and dried milder chiles or chile powder.

Other products take well to the smoker, too: tomatoes, particularly smaller paste varieties, such as Roma, can be halved and smoke-dried. Lightly smoking larger varieties of tomatoes will not necessarily help you preserve them in the pantry, but these can be stored and frozen like roasted tomatoes with a smoky kick: these make the most delicious tomato soup in the known universe.

Fermenting, Pickling, and Other Tricks

I am including a hodge-podge of ideas here that I have used throughout the years to preserve vegetables and fruits. Almost everything I mention here will need to be kept refrigerated or frozen at some point, though almost all here also takes well to canning, should you have the time and resources.

Fermented foods have made a comeback in recent years as the growing consensus suggests that the active cultures, or probiotics, in naturally fermented foods are remarkably good for our overall health, especially in maintaining a healthy digestive system. Pickles that you buy in the supermarket are typically heat-treated in some way or pickled using vinegar and not fermentation; both of these methods effectively kill any active microorganisms. Naturally fermented or "pickled" vegetables made at home contain a host of good probiotics if monitored carefully and taste superior to mass-produced items.

The fermented vegetables collectively known as **kimchi** are no longer an exotic food, thanks to the rapidly growing popularity of Korean food throughout the country. Jars of cabbage kimchi are found on most grocery store shelves but, again, that made at home with your own organic produce is tastier, fresher, and healthier. While some of us may be more familiar with sauerkraut, another traditional fermented cabbage dish, cabbage kimchi is spicier and livelier and fairly simple to make.

To make cabbage kimchi at home, start with brining your cabbage: put a chopped head of cabbage into a brine of 6 cups of water and 3 tablespoons of salt. Weigh the cabbage down with a plate topped by cans and let it sit overnight. The next day, drain cabbage, reserving brine, and mix with half a dozen sliced scallions, half a dozen minced cloves of garlic, a tablespoon or two of grated fresh ginger, and two or three tablespoons of chile powder (gochugaru is the traditional Korean chile powder, but you can, in a pinch, substitute cayenne or other spicy chile powders), and a couple teaspoons of sugar. Make sure the spices coat the cabbage leaves well and pack into sterilized quart jars (I used to use old mayonnaise jars when they were glass; alas, I'd avoid the new plastic ones) and pour over reserved brine just to cover. Put the rest of the reserved brine into sealable plastic baggies and push these into the mouth of the jar; these allow for fermentation bubbles to escape—if you screw a lid on top, the jar will potentially shatter—

while preventing scum from forming on top. Place in a cool dark place (ideally no hotter than 70 degrees: I use the garage in winter) for three to seven days. It will get slightly fizzy and more sour with each day. When it is as sour as you want it—if you're doing this in hot weather, err on the side of sooner rather than later—remove baggies, pouring brine back into the jar, seal, and refrigerate. This will keep for six months or more.

This kimchi method will also work well for radishes, cucumbers, and members of the allium family (I like a mix of leeks, onions, and garlic), and of course, you can customize this basic recipe to suit your tastes. Some kimchi recipes call for the addition of dried shrimp or fish sauce to up the funky ante.

Other kinds of **pickling** calls for vinegar which, while not quite as rich in the probiotic lottery, is still a delicious and healthy way to preserve your harvest. Again, these recipes will need to be kept refrigerated, unless you have canning equipment.

A very basic pickling brine can be made with equal parts vinegar and water with enough salt to both flavor and promote preservation. Many recipes will call for pickling salt which is merely table salt without the iodine; because it is finer than kosher or sea salt, it dissolves in brines more quickly. I myself never bother with it to no detrimental effect. I usually use kosher salt, as it has no additives; you just need to increase the amount called for to compensate for the coarser grains and be sure that it dissolves completely.

So, for example, 2 cups of cider vinegar, 2 cups of water, and 1 tablespoon plus a pinch more of kosher salt makes a great basic pickling liquid for about 2 pints worth of vegetables. Bring brine to a boil, stirring to dissolve the salt, then pour over vegetables packed in sterilized jars. For variety and flavor, add aromatics, such as garlic cloves and dried peppers; add as much sugar as salt for sweet and sour versions; vary the kind of vinegar used. Many vegetables take well to this, including okra and green beans: don't use sugar and do add garlic and peppers. Make sure, if you aren't canning, to blanch these beforehand. For pickled garlic and cucumbers, use the lighter rice wine vinegar and add some sugar. For a lovely blush color and some natural sweetness, add a peeled and sliced beet to some radishes pickled in this manner.

Pickles made in this manner can also be frozen for longer storage.

Other tricks include such things as preserving in oil, vinegar, salt and sugar. All of these elements promote longer storage and/or bring out the flavors of certain suitable produce.

For example, you can make flavored oils. Warm the oil and then gently heat your chosen aromatic in it: herbs, fresh or dried; garlic cloves; chiles, fresh or dried; and/or dried tomatoes. Steep for a day or two, then strain and store in a cool dark place for a couple of months. Other things you can add are citrus peels and whole spices for flavor boosts.

This same method also works for vinegars, though no heating is required and straining isn't always necessary as the acidity in vinegar keeps the produce from spoiling. I particularly enjoy tarragon vinegar, and the delicate flavor of rice wine vinegar preserves the tarragon flavor the best, I think.

Salted vegetables can keep for long periods of time, refrigerated. Simply pack into crocks with layers of salt and fish out bits for use as seasoning. Rinse the salt off and use judiciously as anything kept this way will become intensely salty. Think of preserved lemons or salt-packed capers for examples of what this might entail: salted radishes pack a lovely salty-spicy punch, for one. This method can be used with miso, the fermented soybean paste common in Asian cooking, as well.

Sugar is used in the preservation of fruits that take well to jams and jellies, of course, and I like to make hot pepper jelly at the end of the season on occasion.

Last, a condiment-tonic that I like to keep around in the fridge is **pepper water**. In a sterilized jar, put 4 chopped hot peppers (serrano, jalapeno, Thai, cayenne, or a mix). Add a couple of tablespoons of cider vinegar, a teaspoon each of soy sauce and fish sauce, a bay leaf, and a couple of crushed garlic cloves to your peppers. Bring about 10 ounces of water to a boil then pour over the ingredients in a jar. Let it cool a bit before refrigerating where it will keep indefinitely. Sprinkle it on plain rice; use it to bring some tart heat to soups, stews, curries and the like; add a shot of it to plain tomato juice or a Bloody Mary. Or just have a sip or two of it after dinner.

CHAPTER 7
Sustaining The Seasons: Making The Best Of Your Garden Year Round

While many of these tips and techniques have been briefly discussed in various other chapters, here you will find some specific advice on how to care for your organic garden during each season. Of course, the objective is to garner as much yield as you can throughout the year while also maintaining soil health and sustainability.

Overwintering

There are three things that you can do to provide a healthy winter season for your garden: one, continue to grow appropriate crops; two, plant a cover crop that will both re energize your soil with nutrients and provide warming ground cover; three, mulch the garden well to prevent degradation of topsoil. Or, of course, you can employ a mix of all three.

Crops for overwintering include garlic, onion, and leeks, as discussed in Chapter 3. You can also overwinter certain root vegetable crops such as potatoes, parsnips, and carrots. If you live in regions where winters don't stay too cold for too long—that is, the ground does not stay in a state of hard freeze for an extended period of time—you can also overwinter several varieties of greens such as collards, kale, and heartier varieties of spinach and arugula. Keep in mind, that if you leave crops in the ground for harvesting in the spring, you will need to protect your garden with mulch and be sure to visibly mark where plants are located in order to avoid accidentally digging them up when you turn your garden over for spring planting. Also, be aware that continuously planting can sometimes exhaust your soil: this can be avoided by continuously feeding your garden rich, organic compost or by giving it a winter break and planting an appropriate cover crop.

Cover crops are plants that you grow to promote soil health, not crops you grow to eat. These include field peas, alfalfa, vetch, and some cereal grains (oats, barley, rye, buckwheat). The best crops to choose depend on where you are, what your soil needs, and how long you intend to maintain the cover crop. For a short overwintering, field peas and buckwheat are ideal. Not only do cover crops return nutrients to the soil, but they keep weeds out of competition for garden space, attract beneficial insects, and act as an organic mulch. If your garden seems to produce less one growing season, or if you encounter diseases that are the result of poor soil health, giving your garden a rest with a couple of months of cover crops will rejuvenate. And, when you're ready to turn the garden and plant for spring, your cover crops provide excellent fodder for the compost pile.

If you don't have the time or the inclination to plant during the winter, do your garden the favor of **mulching** well. Mulch also works to keep weeds under control and keeps your soil warm and relatively moist. It also protects any crops that are dormant throughout the winter but will pop up again in spring. Be aware that different mulches will affect your soil in different ways, and seek out organic mulches, of course, from reputable sources. Many biodegradable mulches are readily available and provide the added benefit of being easily tilled back into the soil; these include lawn clippings, raked leaves, or straw. Just be sure that these come from non-chemically treated sources. Wood chip mulches are the most effective at providing winter warmth for your soil; cedar or eucalyptus mulch have the added benefit of being a natural insect repellant. Again, consult your local garden shop, farmers' market, or cooperative extension for specific advice about your region.

Last, be sure to tend to your compost in the winter, as well, adding organic materials to it and making sure it is well covered and continuing to break down.

Preparing for Spring

The first item on your to-do list before the onslaught of the prime growing season is to have your **soil tested**. Find out if your soil is in balance with the right pH (6.5 is ideal) and whether it lacks certain nutrients (or, occasionally, has too much of some). You can do this at home with a soil testing kit, though the information that home kits give you is limited and does not have the advantage of an expert to provide you with advice on how to correct your soil, if necessary. The best place to get your soil tested is at a cooperative extension service if there is one located in your area. If you don't have an extension service near you, there are resources online. Check out the following USDA resources for links. Barring that, consult with a local farmer from your market or a gardening expert in your area.

Next, you'll want to **turn your garden** well, making sure not to disturb any overwintered crops. Here's where you might want a tiller if you have a larger garden. Turning soil breaks up any unwanted roots that may be lurking there as well as aerates the soil and prepares it for planting. Add your compost and organic fertilizer at this time, and be sure that this material is tilled into your garden well before planting.

If the soil in your area isn't conducive for gardening—if it is made up largely of clay, for example—you'll want to **create your topsoil layer** with organically sourced soil. Depending on how large your plot is, you can purchase gardening soil at many large retail outlets—again, look for organic—and gardening shops. This can get expensive if you have a lot of ground to cover, so you can also look to local farmers and/or cooperative extension services to find out where you might purchase soil in bulk. You should only need to do this your first year of gardening, barring some disaster, as the compost you keep should provide you with plenty of healthy new soil to add each year.

This is the time of year that you will typically want to **map out your garden space**, organizing crops according to some basic rules of seasonality, succession planting, and companion planting, with an eye on the practical logistics of space, weed control, and ease of harvest. Herb plants that you will snip throughout the spring and summer should be easy to access, for example, a long, squat raised bed plot should promote ease of harvesting with all crops.

Certainly, spring is the time of year during which you will do much—if not most—of your **planting**. Again, timing is based on your region or agricultural zone (see Chapter 1), but typically, you'll want to direct seed lettuces, greens, radishes, and cruciferous vegetables sometime in early spring, while transplanting seedlings such as tomatoes, herbs, and chile peppers in mid-spring. See

Chapter 3 for advice on how and when to plant a variety of vegetables well-suited to organic gardening.

Sustaining Through the Summer

Summer offers up its own challenges, depending on your region. For most of us, the summers will get hot and dry—to what extent is out of our humble control. This is also the season during which weeds and pests will be at their most prominent, typically speaking. It is also a wonderful time of year when your garden will be at its most productive, so prepare for **regular harvesting and preserving**, if necessary. See Chapter 5 and Chapter 6 for recipe and preservation methods.

Most issues that arise during the summer months are issues that are combated or controlled through preparations that have already been put in place: companion planting to provide shade for plants susceptible to heat, using drip irrigation to provide precise watering to the most important plants when it gets dry, and mulching with appropriate materials to control weeds and keep moisture in the soil.

Be prepared to **visit your garden every day**—once in the morning and once in the evening is ideal—in order to keep up with weeds, pests, and diseases. See Chapter 4 for some more specific advice on dealing with these. Also, be sure to harvest daily: not only do you avoid losing a fruit or vegetable to overgrowth or pest invasion but you also keep the plants healthy and productive.

Extending Into Fall

The concept of **succession planting** cannot be emphasized enough, and as detailed in Chapter 3, several crops that do well in spring can be replanted for an additional fall crop. The more actively you cultivate your garden, the healthier it will be, and while fall presages the cold nearly dormant time of winter, it can be a lovely time to garden. Pests are fewer, weeds die back, and diseases tend to dissipate.

Fall is the ideal time to **plant any crops that you intend to overwinter**, such as garlic, onions, leeks, and various root vegetables or hearty greens. While some of these you will not harvest until the following year (garlic, onions, some root vegetables), you can maximize your harvest by cultivating some fall spinach or other greens to eat through Thanksgiving in certain areas, then cutting the plants back before winter mulching; these will be among the first to poke their green heads up again in spring.

Also consider cruciferous vegetables, some lettuces and greens, and autumn squashes as potential fall crops. One important thing to consider when planting a fall garden is when to plant: it is difficult to germinate seeds in the hot dryness of summer, but your plants need enough time to mature before the first hard freeze of winter. While some plants will survive a frost—and some will even benefit from it in terms of flavor—many will not. If your summers are hot and your autumns are short, it is best to cultivate your seedlings inside for a month or two before transplanting to your garden outdoors.

CHAPTER 8
Imagining Your Impact: The Final Payoff

Now that you have achieved your goal of becoming a successful backyard gardener, take a moment to reflect upon the wide-ranging impact that your efforts have had. Not only are you providing yourself, your family and friends with healthy, nourishing food but you are also reducing your carbon footprint and participating in a movement that promotes sustainability and accountability.

The contemporary American relationship to food is tortured, to say the least. From the inevitability of our *Fast Food Nation* to our passive acceptance of *Dinner at the New Gene Café* to the agonizing deliberation over *The Omnivore's Dilemma* (to use compelling titles of recent books), the reasonably informed consumer might be well justified in throwing up his or her hands in dismay. The corporate takeover of our foodways is no longer limited to the economic dominance of the convenience industry—fast food, supermarket chains, big box marts—and its partners in industrial agriculture, but is also increasingly relegated to scientists and the global giants of genetic engineering. Behind these contentious matters lurks one central theme: the vexed issue of how to produce authentically nutritious and delicious food. Seasonal food, sustainable agriculture, locally grown, preferably organic, produce: these have become the rallying cries of the new resistance. In an age of globalization—asparagus from South America in the dead of winter, even at a Whole Foods market—and in a country where the public discourse continues to confuse even the most conscientious consumer, the problem of how to feed our families well becomes an imperative part of the campaign to restore an ethically compromised system of producing, distributing, and consuming food.

Organically grown food is healthier: there is no other simpler way to say it. It nourishes our bodies and our environment in ways that mass-produced agriculture cannot. Gardening organically means that you are able to grow tastier food with more nutrients within a short walk from your back door. In addition, as we are well aware, organic gardening enriches our soil, our water, and our air by avoiding the use of petrochemicals and instead relying on the creation of a natural microbiome that cycles and recycles its main ingredients in order to continue thriving.

Foremost, your impact hits home—literally. The food that you grow with your own conscientious labor is both more satisfying and more delicious. Most produce that comes out of the agricultural system is bred (or modified) for heartiness and convenience, rather than taste. A bland supermarket tomato or mushy apple have been treated to ship well and to appear attractive without much thought given to the quality of taste or nutritional benefit. It really goes without saying that harvesting your evening meal—even a small part of it—from your own backyard or terrace is immensely pleasurable, both sensually and psychologically.

This also clearly engenders a sense of accountability: if you depend on your soil and your environment for your own food, then you begin to actively support those things, even beyond your own plot of land. This breaks a cycle wherein the corporate control over our foodways feels like our only choice. We have other paths we can choose to take.

Also, consider that your garden is an inspiration. No matter how frustrating gardening may sometimes seem, in those dark moments when the weather is too hot, too cold, too wet, too dry, in the end, it is nothing short of miraculous to create life out of the soil. By engaging in the practice of gardening organically, you provide a role model for your children, your family, your friends, and your neighbors. Good habits have a way of proliferating, and I can tell you from personal experience that, after a couple of seasons gardening in my suburb, I had the pleasure of talking to neighbors from all across the area who would knock on my door to ask advice. I helped a handful of neighbors to set up their own gardens, and I'm certain they inspired more. In what was once a fairly drab neighborhood with clipped lawns, identical hedgerows, and carefully pruned trees became a veritable oasis of gardens—colorful, riotous, delicious, and healthy. Within a few years, a local farmers' market grew out of this. Impacts are powerful in that they create waves of inspiration.

Second, your participation in the relatively simple and enormously satisfying act of gardening organically reverberates beyond the local. It means that you are acknowledging, even if in only a small way, that industrial agriculture isn't necessarily the best thing for human health or the health of the planet. Your decision and desire to garden may not necessarily be an act of rebellion—maybe it is just a fun hobby or a nod to getting healthier—but it is still a small symbol of what might be wrong with a larger system that depends on petrochemicals and relies on science more than it considers the health and well-being of its consumers and its land.

It must be noted that industrial agriculture has brought with it some positives: that we are able to feed more people more consistently and with more convenience is undeniable. But it is also most certainly true that the industry has become politically entrenched and thus wields enormous amounts of power in determining what we eat and how we eat. As many people are aware, only five corporations control the vast majority of our food supply; this results in an increasingly vulnerable population that is held hostage to the decisions made in corporate boardrooms. One small garden plot may not change the world, but it is certainly a start, an acknowledgement of our desires to live in a kinder, gentler, more sustainable world.

Yet, gardening organically is not merely about abstract thinking, it is about getting one's hands dirty, literally, working with the earth and the weather in order to feed the body, the mind, and the soul. It is hard to overestimate the kind of respect one gains for where our food comes from until you've worked a farm or a garden. If your children's only experience of food comes from shrink-wrapped packages or orderly supermarket shelves, then it is unlikely that a strong respect for nature will inherently come out of that. Gardening and farming model the ethics of hard work—reveals the "fruits of our labors," quite literally speaking—and creates strong moral considerations regarding waste and carelessness. It is easy to ignore a shriveling head of lettuce in the fridge if you picked it up for a couple of dollars at a corporate run grocery store; it is nearly impossible to let that go when you planted it, nurtured it, and harvested it yourself.

Not only do we gardeners begin to view waste as an opportunity—compost, anyone?—but we also start to react squeamishly to the sheer amount of plastic that is generated by one trip to the grocery store. Your organic vegetables never see plastic or the inside of a refrigerator truck: a carbon footprint of virtually zero.

On that note, I would like to make a quick aside. Clearly, when gardening on a small plot in the backyard, even when supplemented by trips to the farmers' market, it is unlikely that the grocery store can be completely avoided. Still, yet, we can make choices within that realm that continue to reverberate in some of the same ways as our own choice to garden has. Seek out local producers; avoid out of season produce; buy organic when feasible. Even the largest of grocery store chains—Wal-Mart, for one startling example—have started to carry locally grown or locally made products and have expanded their still somewhat meager organic offerings. If you don't live in a community with a good-sized farmers' market or have access to local, fresh producers, do not despair: you can vote, as they say, with your pocketbook, simply by choosing products that are good for yourself, your family, and your planet.

It is up to us to make small changes in our own lives that impact the larger community and world. As Margaret Mead, the famous anthropologist once said: "Never doubt that a small community of thoughtful, committed citizens can change the world; indeed, it is the only thing that ever has." Our power as consumers lies in not only in our pocketbooks but also in our values. We can do our small part and reach out to others to do theirs.

Though some of the calls to go organic can sometimes be unreasonable—extreme localism is untenable as a way to feed a nation, not to mention a world (remember: our ancestors were hungry much of the time)—there is still much to be gained by engaging in the struggle over the politics of the plate. In the end, there is no one idea or action that can change the history of industrial agriculture but to simply leave it at that is dangerous, a passive invitation to allow more and more genetically modified organisms, processed foods, and corporate control into our grocery stores and homes. It is to divorce ourselves from the communion of the table and to close ourselves off from our neighbors, new and old. To believe that food *has* meaning beyond the purely physical surely paves the way for the creation of a food system that is healthier, more ecologically sound, and ultimately more humane.

Besides, in the end, the food you grow in your backyard tastes really, really good! As well, it is undeniably very good for you and your community. Last, it is truly some of the most satisfying, most enjoyable hard work you will ever do. Taking meals together—breaking bread—represents the best of what humanity has to offer. Bon appetít!

CONCLUSION

From the backyard to the table, organic vegetable gardening from your home is one of the most satisfying and enduring efforts you can undertake. Planning a garden, preparing the soil, nurturing plants, outsmarting pests, harvesting, preserving, and preparing meals are many of the numerous benefits to both body and soul that come out of such an endeavor. Not only are you contributing to the health and well-being of yourself, your friends, and your family, but you are also actively participating in creating a healthier environment and a better world.

I hope you have appreciated this journey through the seasons and now have the confidence and knowledge to begin your own backyard garden. Advice on how to set up a garden; how to prepare the soil; how—and when and what—to plant; how to combat pests and diseases; how to harvest and preserve; how to succession plant to ensure continuous garden growth: these tips, techniques, recipes, and more are all here. In addition, the many positive reasons—from avoiding petrochemicals and their detrimental effects to the fostering of tastier and more nutritious food—for undertaking an organic garden are outlined throughout.

If you have enjoyed this book and learned from its contents, I urge you to take the time to rate this on Amazon. This will lead others to embark upon their own backyard projects, spreading health and happiness, just as your own organic vegetable garden exists as a beacon throughout your wider community.

DESCRIPTION

If you are ready for a fun-filled and deliciously satisfying project to dig into—literally!—then now is the time to embark upon the joyful challenge of growing your own vegetables—organically, healthfully—at home. This book will guide you through the process, from the basics of why and how to the fruitful activities of harvesting and preserving.

Organic Vegetable Gardening gets you started on this journey through the seasons, where you will learn everything from how to tackle the most practical basics to how to cultivate the most enjoyable results. The reasons to grow your own vegetables organically are many and important, from providing personal nourishment to contributing to an ethically sustainable environment.

Some of the tips, techniques, and knowledge you will find in this book includes:

- The Basics of Why and How: not only a compelling list of reasons to propel you into breaking ground for your garden, but also a basic step by step on how to get started
- Soil and Seeds: not only how to coax the best out of your soil, but also specific advice on how to make your own compost bin out of easily acquired materials, as well as tips on how to get the best seeds
- Vegetable Victory: a list of some of the best plants for the organic garden through all the seasons, as well as some information on companion planting and maximizing space
- Preparing for Pests: how to control pests and combat diseases organically
- Healthy Harvest: the basics on weeding and pruning, as well as lots of ideas on how to use all the beautiful produce you grow, including numerous easy recipe methods for each and every plant listed
- Preserving Your Produce: never waste a thing! Canning, freezing, dehydrating, smoking, and fermenting are all ways to extend the life of your harvest, with more recipes to guide you

- Sustaining the Seasons: how to make the most of winter, spring, summer, AND fall
- Imagining Your Impact: taking stock of your accomplishments and appreciating your efforts

The time has never been riper to get your hands dirty with organic vegetable gardening. In the end, you will reap the rewards of these efforts in ways both local and global. To feed your family and friends food that you grow is an immeasurable pleasure, the ultimate act of love, and to do this in a way that supports environmental sustainability is quite literally groundbreaking. Sustenance is more than mere fuel for the body; it is an active fare for the spirit.

www.ingramcontent.com/pod-product-compliance
Lightning Source LLC
Chambersburg PA
CBHW071507070526
44578CB00001B/467